AF454244

The Role of Technology
in Enhancing Supply Chain
Visibility in Africa

Olajumoke Aroyewun

Preface

Supply chains serve as the backbone of economies, facilitating the seamless movement of goods, services, and information across borders, industries, and communities. They are vital to connecting producers with consumers, driving commerce, and sustaining livelihoods. In Africa, these supply chains are not only a testament to the continent's vast potential but also a reflection of its unique challenges. Despite its rich natural resources, dynamic markets, and entrepreneurial spirit, African supply chains are often characterized by inefficiencies, limited visibility, and fragmented infrastructure. Addressing these persistent challenges is not merely a necessity but a significant opportunity to unlock unprecedented economic growth, innovation, and development.

The digital revolution presents an extraordinary chance to reimagine and transform how African supply chains operate. Emerging technologies, including blockchain, artificial intelligence, automation, and the Internet of Things (IoT), are enabling businesses to overcome traditional barriers, optimize processes, and enhance resilience. These tools are opening doors to solutions that were previously unimaginable. However, adopting these technologies requires more than just technical expertise, it demands a strong commitment to sustainability, a spirit of collaboration, and a focus on inclusivity to ensure that no one is left behind in this transformative journey.

This book, *The Role of Technology in Enhancing Supply Chain Visibility in Africa*, is born out of a profound passion for exploring the intersection of technology and development. It aims to illuminate the pathways through which technology can address the complexities and inefficiencies of African supply chains. Through detailed case studies, actionable strategies, and forward-looking insights, this book seeks to provide a comprehensive roadmap for navigating the evolving landscape of supply chain management. Whether you are a seasoned professional, a policymaker seeking solutions, an academic conducting research, or simply a curious learner, this book is designed to offer valuable perspectives and practical knowledge.

Writing this book has been an enriching journey of discovery and learning. It has deepened my appreciation for the intricate dynamics that govern supply chains and highlighted the transformative potential of technology when applied thoughtfully and strategically. My hope is that this work not only informs readers but also inspires meaningful conversations, sparks groundbreaking innovations, and catalyzes actions that will redefine the future of supply chain management across Africa.

As you turn these pages, I invite you to join me on an exploration of how technology is reshaping the present and future of African supply chains. Together, we can envision and build a continent where supply chains are not just efficient but also equitable, sustainable, and empowering; paving the way for a brighter and more inclusive future for generations to come.

Table of Contents

Foreword

Africa is on the cusp of a profound transformation. With its dynamic and youthful population, abundant natural resources, and rapidly expanding digital economy, the continent is uniquely positioned to emerge as a global leader in innovation, commerce, and sustainable development. Yet, realizing this immense potential requires addressing some of Africa's most entrenched challenges, none more critical than the inefficiencies and complexities of its supply chains.

Supply chains are the lifelines of commerce and trade. They form the intricate networks that connect production with consumption, enabling goods, services, and information to flow across regions and borders. In Africa, however, these supply chains face numerous obstacles. Poor infrastructure, fragmented markets, limited visibility, and systemic inefficiencies have long impeded their smooth functioning. These challenges not only constrain economic growth but also perpetuate inequality, reduce competitiveness, and limit opportunities for millions of people across the continent.

In a world increasingly driven by technology, supply chains offer a unique avenue for transformation. Emerging tools and technologies such as blockchain, artificial intelligence (AI), the Internet of Things (IoT), and automation are redefining the way goods and services are produced, distributed, and consumed. For Africa, these technologies represent a chance to leapfrog traditional constraints, build smarter and more efficient supply chains, and foster inclusivity at every stage. By integrating these innovations, African businesses and governments have the opportunity to rethink supply chains as engines of growth, resilience, and equity.

This book, *The Role of Technology in Enhancing Supply Chain Visibility in Africa*, provides an insightful and comprehensive exploration of these possibilities. Olajumoke Aroyewun combines rigorous research, practical analysis, and a visionary outlook to paint a compelling picture of what is possible when technology meets the unique challenges and opportunities of African supply chains. From demystifying complex technologies to presenting real-world applications, this book serves as both a guide and a call to action for those seeking to modernize supply chain operations in Africa.

What sets this book apart is its emphasis on sustainability and inclusivity. It reminds us that true progress cannot be measured solely by efficiency gains or cost reductions. Instead, it must be evaluated through the lens of environmental preservation, social equity, and community empowerment. Africa's transformation is most meaningful when it benefits everyone not just a select few and when it creates a legacy of fairness, responsibility, and opportunity for future generations. By focusing on these critical dimensions, this book challenges us to think beyond profits and logistics and to consider the broader impact of supply chains on societies and ecosystems.

The insights offered in this book are invaluable for anyone invested in Africa's future. Policymakers will find guidance on crafting enabling environments for technology adoption and cross-border collaboration. Entrepreneurs will gain practical strategies for leveraging digital tools to drive competitiveness and growth. Academics and researchers will appreciate the depth of analysis and the framework for future exploration. Most importantly, the book celebrates the resilience, creativity, and determination of Africans to lead the way in shaping a new narrative for global supply chains.

As someone deeply passionate about Africa's economic development, I believe this book is a timely and essential resource. It not only identifies the challenges and opportunities inherent in African supply chains but also provides a vision for overcoming them through innovation, collaboration, and shared purpose. The time to act is now, and the tools are within our reach.

This is more than a book about supply chains; it is a testament to the ingenuity and potential of Africa—a continent that is not merely a participant in the global economy but a leader in defining its future. I invite you to read, reflect, and take action as we collectively build a brighter, more equitable future for all.

Dr. Emmanuel Okafor
Economist and Supply Chain Specialist

About the Author

Olajumoke Aroyewun is a supply chain strategist, technology enthusiast, and advocate for sustainable development. With over a decade of experience in supply chain management across Africa, she has worked extensively with businesses, governments, and development organizations to address inefficiencies, enhance visibility, and drive innovation. Her expertise spans logistics, data analytics, blockchain, and artificial intelligence, making her a sought-after consultant and speaker in the field.

Aroyewun holds a master's degree in Supply Chain Management and Technology Integration from a leading global institution. She is passionate about empowering businesses and communities through technology-driven solutions and has been recognized for her work in promoting sustainability and inclusivity in African supply chains.

Beyond her professional pursuits, Aroyewun is a mentor to young professionals and a vocal advocate for gender equity in technology and business. Her commitment to fostering collaboration and driving change is evident in her writings, which blend rigorous research with actionable insights.

When she's not delving into the complexities of supply chains, Aroyewun enjoys engaging with communities, exploring innovations, and envisioning a future where African supply chains lead the world in efficiency, equity, and sustainability.

This book is a testament to her vision of using technology to unlock Africa's economic potential and create a brighter, more inclusive future.

Introduction

Supply chains are the arteries of commerce, the intricate networks through which goods, services, and information flow to meet the needs of businesses, consumers, and communities. They connect farmers with markets, manufacturers with retailers, and entrepreneurs with global opportunities. In Africa, these networks are uniquely shaped by the continent's vast geographic, cultural, and economic diversity. Yet, they are also constrained by persistent challenges ranging from inadequate infrastructure and fragmented markets to regulatory complexities, environmental pressures, and inefficiencies.

These challenges, while significant, also present immense opportunities for transformation. The global supply chain landscape is rapidly evolving, driven by the emergence of cutting-edge technologies that promise to enhance efficiency, visibility, and resilience. For Africa, this technological revolution represents a chance to leapfrog traditional limitations, modernize operations, and create supply chains that are not only competitive but also sustainable and inclusive.

This book, *The Role of Technology in Enhancing Supply Chain Visibility in Africa*, explores how these transformations are reshaping supply chains across the continent. It begins by examining the unique challenges that African supply chains face, such as unreliable transportation networks, limited access to financing, and fragmented information systems. These issues hinder progress, inflate costs, and limit the continent's ability to fully harness its economic potential. However, they also highlight the critical need for innovation, collaboration, and investment.

The subsequent chapters dive into specific technologies that are driving change. Blockchain, for example, is revolutionizing traceability, ensuring transparency and accountability across the supply chain. The Internet of Things (IoT) is enabling real-time monitoring of goods, enhancing operational efficiency and reducing losses. Artificial intelligence (AI) and data analytics are optimizing decision-making, predicting demand, and mitigating risks. Automation and robotics are improving productivity and reducing costs, while sustainability-focused innovations are addressing environmental concerns and fostering ethical practices.

Throughout the book, I have sought to strike a balance between analysis and action. While it provides a detailed understanding of the technologies transforming supply chains, it also offers practical strategies for implementation. Each chapter includes real-world examples, case studies, and actionable insights, ensuring that readers leave with not just knowledge but also tools to drive meaningful change. This practical focus is particularly important in Africa, where solutions must be adaptable to diverse contexts and scalable to meet the needs of businesses large and small.

Sustainability and inclusivity are central themes of this book. African supply chains are about more than moving goods, they are about empowering communities, fostering innovation, and driving equitable economic growth. By integrating these principles into their operations, businesses can create value not just for themselves but for the wider ecosystem of stakeholders, from farmers and workers to consumers and policymakers. This holistic approach is essential for building resilient supply chains that contribute to long-term prosperity.

Writing this book has been a journey of exploration and learning. It has deepened my appreciation for the challenges and opportunities that define African supply chains and underscored the transformative power of technology when applied thoughtfully and strategically. My hope is that this book inspires readers to embrace the potential of technology, not just as a tool for solving problems but as a catalyst for innovation, inclusion, and sustainability.

This book is written for a diverse audience: supply chain professionals seeking to modernize their operations, policymakers looking to craft enabling environments, entrepreneurs exploring new opportunities, and students curious about the future of commerce in Africa. Regardless of your background, I hope this book equips you with the insights and inspiration to make a difference in your sphere of influence.

Africa's supply chain story is still being written. The continent's challenges are formidable, but so is its resilience, creativity, and capacity for innovation. By leveraging technology, fostering collaboration, and committing to sustainability, we can redefine the future of supply chains not just for Africa, but for the world.

Let us imagine, innovate, and build the supply chains of tomorrow.

1. Understanding Supply Chain Visibility in Africa

Supply chain visibility refers to the seamless tracking and monitoring of goods, processes, and data across all stages of the supply chain, from the sourcing of raw materials to the delivery of finished products to consumers. It is the backbone of modern supply chain management, ensuring that every stakeholder can access accurate and real-time information about the movement and status of goods. In Africa, where logistical challenges and infrastructural deficiencies are prevalent, achieving supply chain visibility presents unique difficulties. However, it also holds the key to unlocking immense economic opportunities and addressing critical inefficiencies across industries.

The African continent's supply chains are highly fragmented, often characterized by multiple intermediaries, poorly integrated systems, and inconsistent processes. These factors create significant barriers to transparency, making it difficult for businesses to track goods in real time or predict disruptions. For example, a manufacturer sourcing raw materials from rural areas in West Africa may face delays due to poor road networks or unexpected regulatory requirements at checkpoints. These disruptions not only increase costs but also impact the reliability and efficiency of supply chains, making visibility a critical priority.

Supply chain visibility enhances efficiency by allowing businesses to streamline their operations and allocate resources more effectively. Real-time tracking ensures that delays or disruptions can be identified and addressed promptly, reducing downtime and optimizing the flow of goods. This is particularly important in industries such as agriculture, where perishable goods must reach their destinations quickly to avoid spoilage. A lack of visibility often results in waste, lost revenue, and missed opportunities for farmers and businesses alike. By implementing systems that provide real-time data on the location and condition of goods, companies can improve their operational efficiency and reduce losses.

The ability to anticipate and mitigate risks is another critical advantage of supply chain visibility. Africa's supply chains are often exposed to a wide range of risks, including political instability, natural disasters, and infrastructure challenges. Without visibility, businesses are left to react to these disruptions after they occur, often at great cost. However, with robust tracking systems and predictive analytics, companies can identify potential risks and take preventive measures. For example, a logistics provider that is aware of a road closure in advance can reroute shipments to avoid delays, ensuring that goods arrive on time and in good condition.

Customer satisfaction is increasingly tied to the level of transparency and reliability that businesses can offer. In today's global marketplace, consumers expect to be informed about the status of their orders at every stage. Businesses that provide real-time updates on shipment progress not only meet customer expectations but also build trust and loyalty. This is particularly important in Africa, where unreliable supply chains often result in delayed deliveries and dissatisfied customers. By leveraging technology to enhance visibility, companies can differentiate themselves in a competitive market and establish a reputation for reliability.

Despite its importance, achieving supply chain visibility in Africa is fraught with challenges. The continent's infrastructure deficit is one of the most significant obstacles. Poorly maintained roads, limited rail networks, and unreliable energy supplies make it difficult to track goods as they move through the supply chain. In rural areas, where connectivity is often limited, the use of digital tools for tracking and monitoring is particularly challenging. These infrastructural issues not only hinder visibility but also increase the cost and complexity of supply chain operations.

Another major challenge is the high cost of implementing advanced technologies such as the Internet of Things (IoT), blockchain, and artificial intelligence. These tools have the potential to revolutionize supply chain visibility, but their adoption requires significant investment in hardware, software, and training. For small and medium-sized enterprises (SMEs), which make up the majority of businesses in Africa, these costs can be prohibitive. Moreover, many companies lack access to affordable financing options that would enable them to invest in these technologies.

Data collection and analysis also pose significant hurdles. In many parts of Africa, supply chain data is still recorded manually, leading to errors and inefficiencies. Even when digital systems are in place, issues such as poor internet connectivity, data silos, and cybersecurity risks can compromise the accuracy and reliability of the information. Without high-quality data, businesses cannot achieve the level of visibility needed to optimize their operations or respond to disruptions effectively.

Cultural and organizational resistance to change further complicates the adoption of supply chain visibility solutions. Many businesses are hesitant to implement new technologies or processes due to a lack of understanding of their benefits or fear of disrupting established workflows. This resistance is often compounded by a lack of technical expertise and training, which makes it difficult for companies to integrate visibility solutions into their operations.

Addressing these challenges requires a comprehensive approach that combines investment in infrastructure, technology, and human capital. Governments and private sector stakeholders must prioritize the development of transportation and communication networks to create an enabling environment for supply chain visibility. For example, investing in better road and rail systems would not only improve the movement of goods but also facilitate the deployment of IoT devices for real-time tracking.

Public-private partnerships can play a critical role in making visibility solutions more accessible to African businesses. By pooling resources and expertise, these partnerships can reduce the cost of implementing advanced technologies and provide training programs to build the necessary skills. For instance, collaborations between technology providers and logistics companies can help SMEs adopt affordable tracking systems that enhance visibility and improve efficiency.

Regulatory reform is also essential for fostering supply chain visibility in Africa. Many countries have complex and inconsistent regulations that complicate cross-border trade and hinder the movement of goods. Simplifying and harmonizing these regulations would not only improve the efficiency of supply chains but also encourage investment in visibility solutions. Regional economic communities such as the African Continental Free Trade Area (AfCFTA) have a critical role to play in promoting regulatory alignment and facilitating the integration of supply chains across the continent.

Raising awareness about the benefits of supply chain visibility is another important step. Many businesses are unaware of how improved visibility can transform their operations and drive growth. Sharing success stories and best practices from organizations that have successfully implemented visibility solutions can help build confidence and encourage adoption. Additionally, governments and industry associations can play a role in promoting visibility as a key driver of economic development and competitiveness.

The economic impact of supply chain visibility in Africa is significant. By improving efficiency, reducing waste, and increasing reliability, visibility solutions can enhance productivity across a wide range of industries. In agriculture, for example, real-time tracking enables farmers to monitor the movement of perishable goods and ensure that they reach markets in optimal condition. This not only reduces food waste but also increases farmers' incomes and strengthens food security.

In manufacturing, supply chain visibility allows companies to optimize production schedules, reduce inventory costs, and respond quickly to changes in demand. Retailers benefit from improved demand forecasting, which helps them maintain optimal stock levels and avoid lost sales due to stockouts or overstocking. At a macroeconomic level, supply chain visibility contributes to economic growth by improving the efficiency of supply chains, reducing costs, and increasing competitiveness. Countries with well-functioning supply chains are better positioned to attract foreign investment and participate in global trade.

Supply chain visibility is not just a tool for improving operational efficiency; it is a catalyst for economic transformation in Africa. By addressing the barriers to adoption and leveraging the power of technology, businesses can unlock the full potential of their supply chains. The benefits of enhanced visibility extend beyond individual organizations, driving growth and development across entire economies. Achieving supply chain visibility is not without its challenges, but the rewards are worth the effort. As Africa continues to embrace digital transformation, supply chain visibility will play a central role in shaping the continent's economic future.

Supply chain visibility does not operate in isolation; it requires a robust ecosystem of technologies, processes, and collaborations to function effectively. For Africa, building this ecosystem is as much about addressing foundational challenges as it is about integrating advanced technologies. One critical area that needs attention is the alignment of stakeholders. Supply chains often involve multiple players, including manufacturers, suppliers, logistics providers, and retailers. Each of these stakeholders has unique priorities and perspectives, which can sometimes conflict, leading to inefficiencies and a lack of trust.

To achieve true visibility, there must be a commitment to transparency and collaboration among all stakeholders. This includes sharing data and insights in real time, ensuring that each player has access to the information they need to make informed decisions. However, achieving this level of transparency requires robust data governance frameworks to address concerns about data security and confidentiality. For instance, a supplier might hesitate to share inventory levels with a retailer due to fears of being exploited in negotiations. Clear policies and agreements can help alleviate these concerns, creating an environment of trust and mutual benefit.

Technological advancements play a pivotal role in enabling supply chain visibility, but they are not a panacea. Tools such as the Internet of Things (IoT) and blockchain can significantly enhance transparency, but their effectiveness depends on how well they are implemented and integrated into existing systems. IoT devices, for example, can be used to monitor the location and condition of goods in transit, providing real-time data that helps businesses respond to issues such as delays, temperature fluctuations, or potential theft. However, deploying IoT devices requires reliable internet connectivity and power sources, which are not always available in many parts of Africa.

Blockchain technology, with its ability to create immutable and transparent records, offers another promising solution for improving supply chain visibility. By using blockchain, businesses can create a single source of truth that all stakeholders can access, reducing disputes and improving accountability. For example, a blockchain-based system could track the journey of a product from the farm to the consumer, ensuring that every step is recorded and verifiable. This is particularly valuable in industries such as agriculture and mining, where there is often a need to demonstrate compliance with ethical and sustainability standards. However, like IoT, blockchain requires significant investment and technical expertise, which can be barriers to adoption for many African businesses.

Education and training are essential components of building supply chain visibility in Africa. Many businesses struggle to adopt new technologies because they lack the skills and knowledge needed to implement and manage these systems. Governments, industry associations, and educational institutions have a role to play in addressing this skills gap. By offering training programs and certifications in supply chain management and technology, they can equip professionals with the expertise needed to drive visibility initiatives. This not only benefits individual businesses but also strengthens the overall competitiveness of Africa's supply chains.

Infrastructure development is another critical area that requires attention. Poor road networks, unreliable rail systems, and congested ports are common challenges that hinder the movement of goods and increase transportation costs. Investments in infrastructure can have a transformative impact on supply chain visibility by enabling smoother and more efficient logistics operations. For example, building better roads and bridges in rural areas can improve access to markets for small-scale farmers, allowing them to transport their produce more quickly and at lower costs. Similarly, upgrading ports and border facilities can reduce delays and streamline cross-border trade, making African supply chains more competitive on the global stage.

Collaboration at the regional level is also vital for improving supply chain visibility in Africa. Many supply chains span multiple countries, and inconsistencies in regulations, customs procedures, and infrastructure can create significant barriers to efficiency. Regional economic communities, such as the East African Community (EAC) and the Southern African Development Community (SADC), can play a crucial role in addressing these issues. By harmonizing regulations, standardizing processes, and investing in shared infrastructure projects, these organizations can facilitate the integration of supply chains across the continent.

The private sector has an equally important role to play in driving supply chain visibility. Large corporations, particularly those with global supply chains, have the resources and expertise to lead by example, demonstrating the benefits of visibility and setting standards for others to follow. For instance, multinational companies operating in Africa can share best practices and provide mentorship to local businesses, helping them adopt visibility solutions and improve their operations. At the same time, SMEs, which make up the majority of businesses in Africa, must be supported with affordable and accessible solutions tailored to their specific needs.

The impact of supply chain visibility extends beyond individual businesses to entire industries and economies. In the healthcare sector, for example, visibility can improve the delivery of essential medicines and medical supplies, ensuring that they reach remote and underserved communities. In the energy sector, it can enhance the management of resources such as oil and gas, reducing waste and increasing efficiency. In retail, visibility can help businesses respond more quickly to changes in consumer demand, reducing stockouts and overstocking.

The social benefits of supply chain visibility are equally significant. By promoting transparency and accountability, visibility solutions can help combat corruption and unethical practices, such as the exploitation of workers or the use of conflict minerals. They can also contribute to environmental sustainability by enabling better tracking and management of resources, reducing waste, and minimizing the carbon footprint of supply chains.

The road to achieving supply chain visibility in Africa is long and challenging, but the potential rewards are immense. By addressing the foundational challenges of infrastructure, technology, and education, and fostering a culture of collaboration and transparency, Africa can build supply chains that are not only more efficient and resilient but also more inclusive and sustainable. The journey toward visibility requires the collective efforts of governments, businesses, and civil society, working together to create a brighter future for the continent.

Supply chain visibility is more than just a business imperative; it is a driver of economic growth, social progress, and environmental sustainability. As Africa embraces digital transformation, visibility will play a central role in shaping the continent's supply chain landscape, unlocking new opportunities and creating a more connected and prosperous future.

1.1 Leveraging Data Analytics for Supply Chain Visibility

Data analytics plays a pivotal role in achieving supply chain visibility, providing businesses with actionable insights that drive decision-making and operational efficiency. In Africa, where supply chain inefficiencies often result from a lack of accurate data, the integration of analytics offers a pathway to significant improvements. Advanced data analytics tools allow organizations to process vast amounts of information collected from various points in the supply chain, such as production facilities, warehouses, and transportation networks.

Predictive analytics, a subset of data analytics, enables companies to forecast demand, optimize inventory levels, and identify potential disruptions before they occur. For example, a retail business in Africa can use historical sales data and market trends to predict future demand for specific products, ensuring that stock levels are adjusted accordingly. This reduces the risk of stockouts or overstocking, both of which can be costly for businesses.

Real-time analytics is another powerful tool for improving supply chain visibility. By analyzing data as it is generated, businesses can monitor the status of goods and respond quickly to any issues that arise. For instance, a logistics company using real-time analytics can detect delays in transportation and reroute shipments to avoid further disruptions. This level of responsiveness is particularly valuable in industries such as healthcare, where timely delivery of medical supplies can save lives.

The adoption of data analytics in Africa's supply chains is still in its early stages, largely due to challenges such as limited access to technology and a shortage of skilled professionals. However, there are promising signs of progress. Governments and private sector players are increasingly investing in digital infrastructure and capacity-building initiatives to promote the use of data analytics. Additionally, the growing availability of cloud-based analytics platforms is making these tools more accessible to small and medium-sized enterprises (SMEs), which form the backbone of Africa's economy.

1.2 The Role of Collaboration in Enhancing Visibility

Collaboration among stakeholders is a cornerstone of effective supply chain visibility. No single organization can achieve full visibility on its own, especially in the complex and interconnected supply chains that characterize Africa. Partnerships between manufacturers, suppliers, logistics providers, and retailers are essential for sharing information and coordinating activities.

One successful example of collaboration can be found in the agricultural sector, where cooperatives have emerged as a model for improving supply chain efficiency. By pooling resources and sharing information, farmers' cooperatives can negotiate better terms with buyers, access real-time market data, and ensure that their products reach markets in a timely manner. This approach not only enhances visibility but also empowers small-scale farmers, who often face significant barriers to market entry.

Technology has a crucial role to play in facilitating collaboration. Digital platforms that connect stakeholders and enable seamless communication are becoming increasingly important. For instance, supply chain management systems that integrate with suppliers' and logistics providers' systems allow businesses to track the movement of goods and monitor inventory levels in real time. These platforms also support collaborative planning and forecasting, helping stakeholders align their activities and reduce inefficiencies.

Cross-border collaboration is particularly important in Africa, where many supply chains span multiple countries. Regional economic communities, such as the African Continental Free Trade Area (AfCFTA), provide a framework for promoting trade and investment across the continent. By simplifying and harmonizing regulations, these organizations can facilitate the integration of supply chains and improve visibility. For example, the establishment of one-stop border posts in East Africa has significantly reduced the time and cost of moving goods across borders, enhancing supply chain efficiency and transparency.

1.3 Driving Innovation Through Local Solutions

Africa's unique challenges call for innovative, context-specific solutions that address the continent's supply chain visibility gaps. Local entrepreneurs and businesses are increasingly stepping up to develop technologies and services tailored to the needs of African markets. These innovations range from mobile-based tracking systems to blockchain-enabled platforms that verify the provenance of goods.

One notable example is the use of mobile technology to improve visibility in last-mile delivery. In many parts of Africa, traditional tracking systems are not feasible due to limited infrastructure and internet connectivity. However, mobile phones, which are widely used across the continent, offer a low-cost and scalable solution. By leveraging SMS-based tracking systems, businesses can provide real-time updates to customers and ensure that goods reach their destinations on time.

Another area of innovation is the development of shared logistics platforms that connect businesses with transportation providers. These platforms optimize the use of available resources by matching shippers with carriers that have unused capacity. This not only reduces transportation costs but also minimizes the environmental impact of supply chain operations. For example, some start-ups in Africa are using artificial intelligence to analyze data and recommend the most efficient routes for deliveries, further enhancing visibility and efficiency.

Investing in local innovation also has the added benefit of creating jobs and building technical expertise within Africa. By supporting homegrown solutions, governments and development organizations can drive economic growth while addressing critical supply chain challenges. Public-private partnerships are particularly effective in this regard, as they combine the resources and expertise of both sectors to develop and scale innovative solutions.

2. The Evolution of Technology in Supply Chains

The history of supply chain technology is a story of continuous innovation and adaptation, driven by the need to optimize operations and meet growing consumer demands. In its earliest forms, supply chain management relied on manual processes and localized systems. Over time, advancements in transportation, communication, and industrial processes laid the foundation for the complex global supply chains we see today. In Africa, the evolution of supply chain technology has followed a unique trajectory, influenced by the continent's infrastructural limitations, economic conditions, and cultural diversity.

During the industrial revolution of the 18th and 19th centuries, technological advancements such as mechanized production, railroads, and steamships transformed global trade and logistics. These innovations enabled businesses to move goods more efficiently, connecting producers and consumers across great distances. However, in Africa, much of the infrastructure developed during this period was built to support colonial economies, focusing on resource extraction rather than the needs of local industries. As a result, early supply chain systems on the continent were fragmented and poorly integrated, with limited focus on efficiency or scalability.

The 20th century brought significant changes to supply chain management with the emergence of new tools and methodologies. Concepts such as just-in-time (JIT) manufacturing and lean production emphasized the importance of reducing waste and improving efficiency, setting the stage for modern supply chain practices. At the same time, advances in transportation and communication, such as the advent of trucks, airplanes, and telephones, further streamlined logistics. While these developments revolutionized supply chains in industrialized regions, their impact in Africa was less pronounced, as many countries were still grappling with post-colonial challenges, including political instability, economic dependency, and inadequate infrastructure.

The digital revolution of the late 20th century marked a turning point in the evolution of supply chain technology. The introduction of computers and enterprise resource planning (ERP) systems allowed businesses to automate key processes, improving accuracy and efficiency. Electronic data interchange (EDI) enabled companies to exchange information seamlessly, reducing delays and errors. Barcoding systems simplified inventory management, making it easier to track goods throughout the supply chain. These innovations transformed supply chains globally, but their adoption in Africa was hindered by limited access to technology and skilled labor. Nonetheless, pockets of progress began to emerge, particularly in industries such as telecommunications and banking, where digital solutions were used to expand reach and improve service delivery.

The advent of e-commerce in the early 2000s further accelerated the adoption of supply chain technology. Platforms such as Amazon and Alibaba set new benchmarks for efficiency, speed, and customer satisfaction, forcing businesses worldwide to invest in technologies that could enhance their operations. In Africa, the rise of e-commerce platforms like Jumia, Konga, and Takealot demonstrated the transformative potential of digital tools in supply chain management. These platforms relied heavily on technology to manage logistics, track deliveries, and provide real-time updates to customers, helping to bridge the gap between businesses and consumers in a continent where traditional retail infrastructure is often underdeveloped.

One of the most significant developments in Africa's supply chain landscape has been the widespread adoption of mobile technology. Mobile phones, which are more accessible than traditional internet infrastructure, have enabled businesses to track goods, communicate with stakeholders, and access market information in real time. Mobile money platforms such as M-Pesa have revolutionized payments, reducing reliance on cash and enabling seamless transactions across supply chains. These innovations have had a particularly profound impact on small-scale traders and farmers, who often face significant barriers to participating in formal supply chains. By providing them with the tools to access markets and financial services, mobile technology has driven inclusion and economic empowerment.

In recent years, Africa has begun to embrace advanced technologies such as the Internet of Things (IoT), blockchain, and artificial intelligence (AI), which are reshaping supply chains globally. IoT devices are being used to monitor the condition and location of goods in transit, providing real-time data that helps businesses optimize storage, transportation, and delivery. Blockchain technology offers a secure and transparent way to record transactions, addressing issues such as fraud and corruption that are prevalent in many African supply chains. For example, blockchain can be used to verify the authenticity of products, ensuring that consumers receive high-quality goods and businesses maintain compliance with ethical standards.

AI and machine learning are enabling businesses to analyze vast amounts of data and generate actionable insights. These technologies are particularly useful for demand forecasting, route optimization, and risk management. For instance, AI-powered platforms can predict delivery delays based on weather conditions or traffic patterns, allowing businesses to adjust their operations proactively. In the healthcare sector, AI is being used to optimize the distribution of medical supplies, ensuring that they reach remote and underserved communities in a timely manner.

Drones and autonomous vehicles represent another frontier in supply chain technology, with the potential to revolutionize last-mile delivery in Africa. Companies like Zipline have already demonstrated the feasibility of drone deliveries in countries such as Rwanda and Ghana, where they are being used to deliver medical supplies to rural areas. These innovations offer a glimpse into the future of supply chain management, where technology overcomes traditional barriers to reach even the most inaccessible locations.

Despite these advancements, the adoption of supply chain technology in Africa remains uneven, with significant disparities between countries and industries. Infrastructure deficits, high costs, and a lack of technical expertise are among the primary barriers to adoption. Many businesses, particularly small and medium-sized enterprises (SMEs), struggle to afford the initial investment required to implement advanced systems. Additionally, inconsistent regulations and bureaucratic hurdles make it difficult for businesses to adopt and scale new technologies across borders.

To overcome these challenges, governments and private sector stakeholders must work together to create an enabling environment for technology adoption. Investments in infrastructure, capacity building, and policy reform are critical to supporting businesses on their journey toward digital transformation. Public-private partnerships can play a key role in providing resources and expertise, while regional economic communities such as the African Continental Free Trade Area (AfCFTA) can promote regulatory harmonization and cross-border collaboration.

The evolution of supply chain technology in Africa is a testament to the continent's resilience and ingenuity. Despite significant obstacles, businesses and entrepreneurs are finding innovative ways to leverage technology to address longstanding inefficiencies and create new opportunities. As Africa continues to embrace digital transformation, the integration of advanced technologies into supply chain operations will be critical for driving growth, enhancing competitiveness, and improving the quality of life for millions of people. This evolution is not just about adopting global trends; it is about creating solutions that are uniquely African, designed to meet the needs and aspirations of the continent's diverse and dynamic markets.

The pace of technological evolution in supply chains is accelerating, with Africa finding itself at a crossroads between adapting global innovations and crafting localized solutions. This unique position has given rise to creative approaches tailored to address the continent's distinct challenges, such as limited infrastructure, fragmented markets, and a predominantly informal economy. The interplay between these challenges and opportunities continues to shape the trajectory of supply chain technology in Africa.

One of the critical factors driving technological advancement in African supply chains is the increasing availability of affordable technology. In the past, the high cost of adopting advanced systems such as enterprise resource planning (ERP) software or radio-frequency identification (RFID) technology excluded many businesses, particularly small and medium-sized enterprises (SMEs), from leveraging these tools. However, recent advancements in cloud computing and the proliferation of open-source software have democratized access to these solutions. Today, even small-scale businesses can implement cloud-based inventory management systems or track goods using mobile-enabled GPS technologies, leveling the playing field and opening new avenues for growth.

Another significant driver of supply chain innovation in Africa is the growing emphasis on public-private partnerships (PPPs). Governments across the continent are increasingly recognizing the importance of robust supply chains for economic development and are working with private sector stakeholders to modernize logistics and infrastructure. For example, PPPs have played a critical role in expanding port facilities, building better road networks, and deploying smart technologies in customs and border management systems. By integrating digital platforms into these systems, stakeholders can reduce delays, enhance transparency, and facilitate smoother cross-border trade.

Technology is also transforming supply chain financing, an area that has historically been a bottleneck for African businesses. Traditional financing models, which rely on collateral and stringent credit requirements, have excluded many small businesses from accessing the capital needed to scale their operations. Fintech innovations are bridging this gap by offering alternative financing solutions that leverage technology to assess creditworthiness. For instance, platforms that use transaction data from mobile money or digital marketplaces to evaluate a business's financial health are enabling SMEs to secure loans and invest in supply chain improvements. These solutions are not only making supply chains more efficient but also fostering financial inclusion and economic empowerment.

As Africa's economies become more integrated, regional trade initiatives such as the African Continental Free Trade Area (AfCFTA) are providing a strong impetus for supply chain modernization. By reducing tariffs and harmonizing regulations, AfCFTA aims to create a single market for goods and services across 54 African countries. This initiative has the potential to significantly enhance supply chain efficiency by eliminating trade barriers and encouraging investment in regional infrastructure. However, realizing this vision requires robust technological systems that can handle the complexities of cross-border trade, such as customs documentation, compliance tracking, and real-time shipment monitoring.

The role of education and capacity building in supporting supply chain technology adoption cannot be overstated. A significant barrier to technological progress in Africa's supply chains is the lack of skilled professionals who can implement and manage advanced systems. Universities, vocational training institutes, and industry associations are stepping up to address this gap by offering specialized courses and certifications in supply chain management, logistics, and technology. These programs are equipping the next generation of supply chain professionals with the knowledge and skills needed to drive innovation and efficiency across the continent.

In addition to formal education, informal training programs and peer-to-peer learning are gaining traction as effective ways to disseminate knowledge and best practices. For example, initiatives that bring together supply chain professionals to share insights and collaborate on common challenges are fostering a culture of innovation and continuous improvement. Technology-focused events, such as hackathons and innovation labs, are also providing a platform for entrepreneurs and developers to create and test solutions that address specific pain points in African supply chains.

The cultural context of Africa also plays a significant role in shaping the adoption and evolution of supply chain technology. In many parts of the continent, informal networks and relationships form the backbone of supply chains. While this can create challenges for transparency and scalability, it also presents opportunities to leverage these networks as a foundation for technology adoption. For example, digital platforms that build on existing community structures, such as cooperatives or informal trade associations, can achieve faster adoption and greater impact by aligning with local customs and practices.

The rise of social enterprises and impact-driven organizations in Africa is another factor contributing to the evolution of supply chain technology. These organizations are leveraging technology not only to optimize operations but also to address pressing social and environmental challenges. For instance, startups that focus on last-mile delivery solutions are improving access to essential goods in remote areas, while those that specialize in circular supply chains are promoting sustainability by reducing waste and encouraging recycling. By integrating social impact into their business models, these organizations are demonstrating that supply chain technology can be a force for good.

As Africa continues to navigate its technological evolution, the need for localized solutions that address the continent's unique challenges becomes increasingly apparent. While global technologies such as blockchain, IoT, and AI offer immense potential, their implementation must be adapted to the realities of African markets. This requires a deep understanding of local contexts, as well as collaboration between governments, businesses, and communities. By fostering an environment of innovation and inclusivity, Africa can not only catch up with global supply chain trends but also lead the way in developing solutions that are relevant and scalable.

The evolution of technology in supply chains is not just a story of progress but also a testament to the resilience and ingenuity of the people and organizations driving this change. In Africa, where challenges are often more pronounced, the achievements in supply chain technology represent a beacon of hope and a blueprint for the future. By continuing to invest in technology, build capacity, and foster collaboration, Africa has the opportunity to transform its supply chains into engines of growth and development, creating a more connected and prosperous continent for generations to come.

2.1 The Intersection of Sustainability and Supply Chain Technology

In recent years, the push for sustainability has significantly influenced the development and adoption of supply chain technology. The growing awareness of environmental, social, and governance (ESG) considerations has compelled businesses to rethink their supply chain strategies. For Africa, where environmental challenges such as deforestation, water scarcity, and climate change disproportionately affect communities, sustainability is not just a business priority but a necessity for long-term survival.

Technology plays a crucial role in helping African businesses adopt sustainable practices within their supply chains. Tools such as carbon tracking software and IoT sensors allow companies to measure and monitor the environmental impact of their operations in real time. For example, logistics providers can use route optimization algorithms to minimize fuel consumption and reduce greenhouse gas emissions, while manufacturers can implement smart energy systems to lower their carbon footprints.

Blockchain technology offers unique advantages in promoting supply chain sustainability by providing transparency and accountability. By using blockchain, businesses can create immutable records of their sourcing and production processes, ensuring compliance with ethical and environmental standards. This is particularly relevant in Africa's extractive industries, such as mining, where there is a growing demand for responsibly sourced materials. Blockchain can verify that minerals are conflict-free and meet international certification standards, enhancing trust and competitiveness in global markets.

Another critical area where sustainability intersects with technology is waste reduction. Circular supply chains, which emphasize recycling, reuse, and resource efficiency, are gaining traction in Africa. Technology is enabling businesses to track waste streams, identify opportunities for repurposing materials, and develop closed-loop systems that minimize environmental impact. For example, start-ups in the fashion industry are using digital platforms to connect textile waste producers with recycling companies, creating value from materials that would otherwise end up in landfills.

While these advancements are promising, achieving widespread adoption of sustainable supply chain technologies in Africa requires significant investment and policy support. Governments can play a pivotal role by offering incentives for businesses to adopt green technologies, such as tax breaks or subsidies for renewable energy projects. Additionally, partnerships with international organizations and NGOs can provide the technical expertise and funding needed to scale these initiatives. Sustainability must become an integral part of supply chain strategies, supported by technology and driven by collaboration across sectors.

2.2 Resilience Through Digital Transformation

The importance of resilience in supply chain operations has been underscored by recent global events, such as the COVID-19 pandemic and geopolitical disruptions, which have highlighted vulnerabilities in supply chains worldwide. In Africa, where supply chains are often fragile due to infrastructural and logistical challenges, the need for resilience is even more pronounced. Digital transformation offers a pathway to building more robust and adaptable supply chains that can withstand shocks and disruptions.

One of the key enablers of supply chain resilience is data-driven decision-making. Digital tools that provide real-time visibility into supply chain operations empower businesses to identify risks and respond proactively. For example, during the

COVID-19 pandemic, companies that had invested in digital platforms were better equipped to monitor disruptions, such as factory closures or transportation delays, and adjust their strategies accordingly. This ability to pivot quickly and efficiently is essential for maintaining continuity in uncertain environments.

Another critical aspect of resilience is supply chain diversification. Overreliance on a single supplier or transportation route can create bottlenecks and increase vulnerability to disruptions. Technology can help businesses identify and evaluate alternative suppliers, routes, and logistics partners, ensuring that they have multiple options in place. Platforms that aggregate supplier data and provide insights into performance, capacity, and risk factors are particularly valuable in this regard, enabling businesses to make informed choices and mitigate dependency risks.

Automation is also a powerful tool for enhancing supply chain resilience. By automating repetitive and time-consuming tasks, businesses can reduce their reliance on manual labor and minimize the risk of human error. In industries such as agriculture and manufacturing, automation technologies such as drones, robotic process automation (RPA), and autonomous vehicles are improving efficiency and reliability. For example, drones are being used to monitor crop health and deliver agricultural inputs in remote areas, ensuring continuity even in the face of labor shortages or logistical challenges.

The role of partnerships and ecosystems in building resilient supply chains cannot be overlooked. Collaboration between businesses, governments, and technology providers is essential for creating the infrastructure and frameworks needed to support digital transformation. Regional initiatives, such as the African Continental Free Trade Area (AfCFTA), provide a platform for fostering cross-border collaboration and investment in supply chain resilience. By working together, stakeholders can address systemic issues such as poor infrastructure, regulatory fragmentation, and skills gaps, creating a more conducive environment for digital innovation.

However, achieving resilience through digital transformation is not without its challenges. The cost of technology remains a significant barrier for many African businesses, particularly SMEs. Additionally, the lack of reliable internet connectivity and energy infrastructure in some regions limits the effectiveness of digital tools. Addressing these challenges requires a holistic approach that combines investment in technology with capacity-building initiatives and policy reform. Governments must prioritize digital infrastructure development, while businesses and development partners must work together to provide affordable and scalable solutions.

3. Digital Transformation in African Supply Chains

Digital transformation has become a cornerstone for businesses seeking to thrive in today's interconnected global economy. In Africa, where traditional supply chains are often plagued by inefficiencies, delays, and fragmentation, digital transformation represents an opportunity to revolutionize operations and bridge long-standing gaps. The integration of digital technologies into supply chain processes not only enhances efficiency but also enables businesses to adapt to changing market demands and external disruptions. This chapter examines the role of digital transformation in reshaping African supply chains, the technologies driving this shift, and the challenges that must be addressed to unlock its full potential.

Digital transformation begins with the digitization of supply chain operations. Many African businesses still rely on manual processes and paper-based systems, which are prone to errors and delays. Digitization involves replacing these traditional methods with digital tools that automate and streamline tasks, such as inventory management, order processing, and shipment tracking. For example, a warehouse that adopts a cloud-based inventory management system can monitor stock levels in real time, reducing the risk of overstocking or stockouts. Similarly, digital platforms that track the movement of goods across transportation networks enable businesses to identify bottlenecks and optimize delivery routes.

The Internet of Things (IoT) is one of the most transformative technologies driving digital transformation in African supply chains. IoT devices, such as sensors and trackers, provide real-time data on the location, condition, and movement of goods. In industries like agriculture, IoT sensors can monitor temperature and humidity levels during the transportation of perishable goods, ensuring that they arrive in optimal condition. This is particularly important in Africa, where inadequate cold chain infrastructure often leads to significant post-harvest losses. By leveraging IoT technology, businesses can enhance visibility and control across the supply chain, reducing waste and improving efficiency.

Blockchain technology is another key enabler of digital transformation, offering a secure and transparent way to record and verify transactions. For African supply chains, where issues such as fraud, counterfeiting, and corruption are common, blockchain provides a solution to enhance trust and accountability. For example, blockchain can be used to create a digital ledger that tracks the journey of goods from the source to the end consumer, ensuring that every step of the process is documented and verifiable. This is particularly valuable in sectors such as mining and agriculture, where there is growing demand for ethically and sustainably sourced products.

Artificial intelligence (AI) and machine learning are revolutionizing supply chain management by enabling businesses to analyze vast amounts of data and generate actionable insights. AI-powered algorithms can predict demand patterns, optimize inventory levels, and recommend the most efficient delivery routes. For example, a logistics company using AI can anticipate delays caused by weather conditions or traffic congestion and proactively adjust its operations to minimize disruptions. In Africa, where supply chains are often vulnerable to external shocks, such predictive capabilities are invaluable for maintaining continuity and resilience.

Digital marketplaces and e-commerce platforms are also driving digital transformation in African supply chains, connecting businesses with consumers and suppliers more effectively. Platforms like Jumia and Konga have created ecosystems that facilitate seamless transactions, logistics, and customer service. These platforms leverage digital tools to manage inventory, track deliveries, and provide real-time updates, enhancing transparency and efficiency. Additionally, digital marketplaces are empowering small and medium-sized enterprises (SMEs) by giving them access to broader markets and enabling them to compete on a level playing field with larger players.

While the benefits of digital transformation are clear, its implementation in African supply chains is not without challenges. One of the primary barriers is the lack of digital infrastructure in many parts of the continent. Poor internet connectivity, unreliable power supply, and inadequate transportation networks limit the effectiveness of digital tools and hinder their adoption. For example, a business in a rural area with intermittent internet access may struggle to use cloud-based platforms or IoT devices, undermining its ability to fully digitize its operations.

The high cost of technology is another significant obstacle. Advanced digital tools, such as AI-powered analytics platforms or blockchain systems, often require substantial investment in hardware, software, and training. For many African businesses, particularly SMEs, these costs are prohibitive. Additionally, the lack of access to affordable financing options makes it difficult for businesses to invest in digital transformation initiatives.

Capacity building and skills development are critical for ensuring the success of digital transformation in African supply chains. Many businesses lack the technical expertise needed to implement and manage digital technologies effectively. This skills gap is particularly pronounced in rural and underserved areas, where access to training and education is limited. Addressing this challenge requires a concerted effort from governments, educational institutions, and industry players to provide training programs and resources that equip professionals with the knowledge and skills needed for digital transformation.

Despite these challenges, there are promising examples of successful digital transformation in African supply chains. In Kenya, Twiga Foods has leveraged digital technology to streamline the distribution of fresh produce, connecting farmers directly with retailers and reducing post-harvest losses. In South Africa, logistics companies are using IoT-enabled tracking systems to monitor the movement of goods and optimize delivery routes, improving efficiency and reducing costs. These success stories demonstrate the potential of digital transformation to drive positive change across the continent's supply chains.

The role of governments and policy makers is critical in facilitating digital transformation. By creating an enabling environment through supportive policies, investments in infrastructure, and incentives for technology adoption, governments can accelerate the pace of digital transformation in African supply chains. For example, public-private partnerships can be used to build digital infrastructure, such as broadband networks and data centers, that support the adoption of advanced technologies. Additionally, policies that promote innovation and entrepreneurship can encourage the development of localized solutions that address Africa's unique supply chain challenges.

Digital transformation is not just a technological shift; it is a cultural and organizational change that requires businesses to rethink their processes, workflows, and strategies. For African supply chains, this transformation is both a challenge and an opportunity. By embracing digital technologies and fostering a culture of innovation, businesses can build supply chains that are more efficient, resilient, and sustainable. The journey toward digital transformation may be complex, but the rewards are immense, offering the potential to unlock new opportunities and drive economic growth across the continent.

The successful digital transformation of African supply chains requires more than just adopting advanced tools; it also involves reimagining how businesses interact with one another and their customers. At the heart of this transformation is the concept of interconnected ecosystems, where every stakeholder from producers to consumers plays a role in creating seamless, efficient, and transparent supply chains. These ecosystems are enabled by digital platforms that facilitate real-time communication, data sharing, and collaboration across the supply chain.

One of the most significant benefits of interconnected ecosystems is their ability to foster inclusivity. In Africa, where informal markets and small-scale enterprises dominate many industries, digital platforms can help bridge the gap between informal and formal supply chains. For example, a digital marketplace that connects smallholder farmers with buyers not only provides them with access to broader markets but also integrates them into formal supply chains, enabling them to benefit from standardized pricing, quality assurance, and financial services. This inclusivity is critical for driving economic empowerment and reducing inequality across the continent.

The role of mobile technology in enabling digital ecosystems cannot be overstated. Mobile phones are ubiquitous in Africa, with penetration rates surpassing those of traditional internet infrastructure in many regions. This accessibility makes mobile technology a powerful tool for digitizing supply chains and expanding access to underserved populations. For instance, mobile apps that allow small-scale traders to list their products, track inventory, and receive payments electronically are transforming how businesses operate in rural and remote areas. These solutions are not only making supply chains more efficient but also fostering entrepreneurship and innovation at the grassroots level.

In addition to enhancing inclusivity, digital transformation also drives greater transparency and accountability in supply chains. By leveraging technologies such as blockchain, businesses can create immutable records of transactions, ensuring that every step of the supply chain is documented and verifiable. This transparency is particularly valuable in industries where trust is a critical issue, such as agriculture, mining, and healthcare. For example, blockchain can be used to verify the authenticity of pharmaceutical products, reducing the prevalence of counterfeit drugs and ensuring that patients receive safe and effective treatments.

Transparency also extends to environmental and social impacts, enabling businesses to meet the growing demand for ethical and sustainable practices. Consumers and investors are increasingly holding companies accountable for their environmental footprints and labor practices, creating a strong incentive for businesses to adopt transparency-enhancing technologies. In Africa, where issues such as deforestation, water scarcity, and exploitation are pressing concerns, supply chain transparency can play a pivotal role in promoting sustainability and social responsibility. For example, a coffee exporter using blockchain to track the origin of its beans can demonstrate compliance with fair trade standards, enhancing its appeal to conscious consumers and markets.

Collaboration is another cornerstone of digital transformation, and its importance cannot be understated in the African context. Many of the continent's supply chain challenges, such as inadequate infrastructure and regulatory fragmentation, are systemic issues that require collective action. By fostering collaboration among stakeholders, digital platforms can help businesses overcome these challenges and create more resilient supply chains. For example, a logistics company that partners with local transportation providers and customs agencies can streamline cross-border trade, reducing delays and costs for all parties involved.

Digital transformation also provides businesses with the tools to enhance customer engagement and satisfaction. Real-time tracking systems, for instance, allow customers to monitor the status of their orders, providing them with greater visibility and peace of mind. In the e-commerce sector, platforms that offer personalized recommendations and seamless payment options are enhancing the shopping experience and building customer loyalty. These innovations are particularly important in Africa, where consumer trust is often a barrier to online transactions. By improving transparency and reliability, digital technologies can help businesses build stronger relationships with their customers and expand their reach.

Despite these benefits, the journey toward digital transformation is not without challenges. One of the most significant obstacles is the digital divide, which continues to limit access to technology for many businesses and communities. Bridging this divide requires targeted investments in digital infrastructure, such as broadband networks and data centers, as well as initiatives to make technology more affordable and accessible. Governments and development organizations have a critical role to play in addressing these disparities, ensuring that digital transformation benefits everyone, not just a privileged few.

Another challenge is the need for cultural and organizational change. Digital transformation requires businesses to rethink their processes, workflows, and mindsets, which can be a daunting task for organizations that are deeply rooted in traditional practices. Overcoming this resistance to change requires strong leadership and a clear vision for the future. Business leaders must communicate the value of digital transformation to their teams, provide training and support, and foster a culture of innovation and adaptability.

The role of education and capacity building in supporting digital transformation cannot be overstated. Many African businesses lack the technical expertise needed to implement and manage digital technologies effectively. Addressing this skills gap requires a multi-pronged approach, including formal education, vocational training, and on-the-job learning opportunities. Industry associations and technology providers can also play a role by offering certifications and training programs that equip professionals with the knowledge and skills needed to succeed in a digital economy.

The future of digital transformation in African supply chains is bright, but it will require sustained effort and collaboration to unlock its full potential. As businesses, governments, and development partners work together to overcome barriers and seize opportunities, they will lay the foundation for a more connected, efficient, and inclusive supply chain ecosystem. The integration of digital technologies into supply chains is not just about improving operations; it is about creating a better future for Africa, where businesses and communities thrive together in a digitally empowered world.

3. 1 Localized Solutions for Unique African Challenges

Africa's diverse geography, cultural dynamics, and infrastructural disparities necessitate localized approaches to digital transformation in supply chains. While global solutions often provide a starting point, their implementation must be adapted to fit the unique conditions of the continent. For instance, rural areas with limited internet access and unreliable power grids require solutions that prioritize simplicity and offline functionality. Mobile-based platforms that operate using SMS or USSD, rather than relying on internet connectivity, have proven effective in bridging the gap between technology and accessibility.

Localized solutions also play a vital role in addressing Africa's informal economy, which accounts for a significant portion of supply chain activities across the continent. Informal traders, small-scale producers, and unregistered businesses are often excluded from formal supply chains due to a lack of documentation or compliance with regulatory requirements. Digital platforms tailored to these groups can help integrate them into formal supply chains while respecting their unique operational models. For example, a digital tool that allows informal traders to register and track their goods without extensive paperwork can facilitate participation in broader markets, fostering growth and inclusivity.

Agriculture, which is the backbone of many African economies, provides a powerful case for the importance of localized solutions. Many farmers face challenges such as post-harvest losses, market access barriers, and a lack of price transparency. Digital platforms designed for agriculture, such as e-extension services and crop monitoring apps, address these issues by providing farmers with real-time weather updates, market price trends, and advice on best practices. Additionally, supply chain management tools that connect farmers directly with buyers eliminate intermediaries, ensuring fair pricing and reducing inefficiencies.

Logistics companies operating in Africa are also leveraging localized solutions to navigate complex transportation networks and address the continent's unique challenges. Route optimization tools that incorporate local knowledge, such as informal transit points or seasonal road conditions, are helping businesses improve delivery times and reduce costs. In remote areas where traditional delivery vehicles are impractical, companies are exploring innovative solutions such as motorcycle-based couriers or drone deliveries. These localized approaches not only enhance efficiency but also demonstrate the adaptability and ingenuity of African businesses in overcoming logistical hurdles.

3.2 The Role of Policy and Regulation in Digital Transformation

Policy and regulatory frameworks play a critical role in shaping the landscape for digital transformation in African supply chains. Supportive policies that promote innovation, investment, and fair competition are essential for creating an environment where businesses can thrive. Governments across the continent are increasingly recognizing the importance of digital transformation and are implementing strategies to drive its adoption. However, inconsistent regulations, bureaucratic red tape, and protectionist policies still pose significant challenges.

One of the key areas where policy intervention is needed is in the harmonization of cross-border trade regulations. Many African supply chains span multiple countries, but discrepancies in customs procedures, documentation requirements, and tariffs create barriers to efficiency. Regional economic communities, such as the African Continental Free Trade Area (AfCFTA), are working to address these issues by establishing common standards and simplifying trade processes. For example, the implementation of one-stop border posts in East Africa has significantly reduced clearance times for goods, improving the flow of trade across the region.

Data privacy and security are also critical considerations in the digital transformation of supply chains. As businesses increasingly rely on digital platforms to manage their operations, the need for robust data protection frameworks becomes more urgent. Governments must strike a balance between enabling innovation and protecting sensitive information, ensuring that businesses and consumers can trust digital systems. For instance, policies that mandate encryption standards and require companies to report data breaches can enhance security while fostering confidence in digital technologies.

Access to financing is another area where policy interventions can accelerate digital transformation. Many African businesses, particularly SMEs, struggle to secure the capital needed to invest in advanced technologies. Governments can address this issue by creating funding mechanisms, such as grants, low-interest loans, or tax incentives, that encourage businesses to adopt digital solutions. Additionally, partnerships with international organizations and development banks can provide the financial support needed to scale digital transformation initiatives across the continent.

Education and capacity building must also be central to policy efforts. Many African countries face a significant skills gap in technology and supply chain management, which hinders the effective implementation of digital solutions. By investing in education and training programs, governments can equip the workforce with the skills needed to drive digital transformation. For example, initiatives that incorporate digital literacy into school curricula or offer vocational training in logistics and technology can build a pipeline of talent to support the continent's evolving supply chains.

Collaboration between the public and private sectors is essential for addressing these policy and regulatory challenges. Governments, businesses, and industry associations must work together to identify pain points, develop practical solutions, and ensure that policies are aligned with the needs of the market. For example, multi-stakeholder dialogues that bring together policymakers, technology providers, and supply chain professionals can foster a shared understanding of priorities and create a roadmap for digital transformation.

4. The Role of Artificial Intelligence and Machine Learning in Supply Chains

Artificial intelligence (AI) and machine learning (ML) are revolutionizing supply chains worldwide, and Africa is beginning to tap into their transformative potential. These advanced technologies have the power to analyze vast amounts of data, optimize operations, and predict future outcomes, making supply chains more efficient, agile, and resilient. In a continent where supply chain inefficiencies often hinder economic growth, AI and ML offer innovative solutions to longstanding challenges, from improving inventory management to reducing transportation costs.

AI and ML differ in their applications but are closely related. AI refers to the broader concept of machines performing tasks that typically require human intelligence, such as decision-making and problem-solving. ML, a subset of AI, involves teaching machines to learn and improve from experience without being explicitly programmed. Together, these technologies can enhance every aspect of supply chain management, from planning and procurement to production and distribution.

One of the most impactful applications of AI in African supply chains is demand forecasting. Traditional methods of predicting demand often rely on historical sales data, which can be inaccurate or incomplete. AI-powered algorithms, on the other hand, analyze a wide range of variables, including market trends, consumer behavior, weather patterns, and economic indicators, to provide more accurate forecasts. For example, a retailer in Africa can use AI to predict which products are likely to sell during a specific season or in response to a marketing campaign, enabling them to stock inventory more effectively and reduce waste.

In logistics and transportation, AI is playing a crucial role in route optimization. By analyzing traffic patterns, weather conditions, and delivery schedules, AI-powered systems can recommend the most efficient routes for vehicles, reducing fuel consumption and delivery times. This is particularly valuable in Africa, where poor road infrastructure and unpredictable traffic conditions often disrupt supply chains. For example, a logistics company delivering goods in Lagos, Nigeria, can use AI to navigate the city's notorious traffic jams, ensuring timely deliveries and minimizing costs.

Machine learning is also transforming warehouse management by automating processes and improving efficiency. ML algorithms can analyze data from warehouse operations to identify bottlenecks, optimize storage layouts, and streamline picking and packing processes. In e-commerce, where speed and accuracy are critical, these capabilities can significantly enhance customer satisfaction. For instance, an online retailer in South Africa can use ML to predict peak shopping periods and allocate resources accordingly, ensuring that orders are processed and shipped without delays.

Another promising application of AI and ML in African supply chains is risk management. Supply chains are inherently vulnerable to disruptions, whether caused by natural disasters, political instability, or economic volatility. AI-powered systems can analyze historical data and real-time information to identify potential risks and recommend mitigation strategies. For example, during the COVID-19 pandemic, businesses that leveraged AI were better able to anticipate disruptions in their supply chains and adjust their operations to minimize the impact. In agriculture, AI can predict crop failures due to droughts or pests, enabling farmers to take preventive measures and protect their livelihoods.

AI and ML are also enhancing supply chain visibility, a critical challenge for many African businesses. By integrating data from various sources, such as IoT devices, sensors, and GPS trackers, AI systems provide real-time insights into the movement and condition of goods. This visibility enables businesses to monitor inventory levels, track shipments, and respond quickly to delays or disruptions. For instance, a cold chain logistics provider transporting perishable goods across Kenya can use AI to monitor temperature conditions and ensure that products remain fresh throughout the journey.

In addition to optimizing existing operations, AI and ML are driving innovation in supply chain design. By simulating different scenarios and analyzing their outcomes, these technologies help businesses identify the most efficient and cost-effective supply chain structures. For example, a manufacturer in Ethiopia can use AI to determine the optimal location for a new distribution center, taking into account factors such as proximity to suppliers, transportation costs, and customer demand.

Despite their potential, the adoption of AI and ML in African supply chains faces significant challenges. One of the primary barriers is the lack of technical expertise and skilled professionals to develop and manage these technologies. Many businesses lack the in-house capabilities needed to implement AI-powered systems, while external service providers are often expensive or inaccessible. Addressing this skills gap requires targeted investments in education and training programs that equip professionals with the knowledge and tools to leverage AI and ML effectively.

Another challenge is the cost of implementing AI and ML solutions. Advanced systems often require significant investment in hardware, software, and data infrastructure, which can be prohibitive for small and medium-sized enterprises (SMEs). Additionally, the availability of high-quality data is a critical prerequisite for the success of AI and ML systems. In many African countries, data is often siloed, incomplete, or unreliable, making it difficult to train algorithms and generate meaningful insights.

To overcome these challenges, governments and private sector stakeholders must collaborate to create an enabling environment for AI and ML adoption. Public-private partnerships can play a crucial role in funding AI initiatives and building the necessary infrastructure. For example, governments can establish innovation hubs that provide businesses with access to AI tools, training programs, and technical support. Similarly, technology providers can offer affordable and scalable solutions tailored to the needs of African businesses.

The ethical implications of AI and ML must also be considered, particularly in the context of data privacy and algorithmic bias. As businesses increasingly rely on these technologies to make decisions, it is essential to ensure that they operate transparently and equitably. Governments can play a role by establishing regulatory frameworks that promote responsible AI use, protecting the rights of consumers and employees while encouraging innovation.

The transformative potential of AI and ML in African supply chains is immense, offering solutions to some of the continent's most pressing challenges. By improving efficiency, reducing costs, and enhancing visibility, these technologies can drive significant economic growth and create new opportunities for businesses and communities. However, realizing this potential requires a concerted effort to address the barriers to adoption and ensure that the benefits of AI and ML are widely distributed.

AI and ML are not only transforming operational aspects of supply chains but are also driving strategic decision-making at a scale previously unimaginable. These technologies have enabled businesses to transition from reactive to proactive and even predictive approaches, fundamentally altering how supply chains are managed in Africa. By leveraging AI and ML, companies can identify opportunities for growth, improve stakeholder collaboration, and develop more sustainable and resilient supply chain models.

One of the emerging applications of AI in African supply chains is in supplier relationship management. Traditionally, supplier selection and performance evaluation have been manual, time-consuming processes prone to bias and error. AI-powered platforms, however, can analyze vast datasets to assess supplier reliability, quality, and financial stability. For instance, a manufacturer sourcing raw materials across multiple African countries can use AI to rank suppliers based on factors such as delivery times, defect rates, and price competitiveness. This level of insight not only improves supplier selection but also strengthens relationships by identifying opportunities for mutual benefit, such as co-investment in technology or capacity building.

Machine learning is also proving invaluable in enhancing the customer experience. Personalized recommendations, dynamic pricing, and tailored promotions are increasingly becoming the norm in industries like retail and e-commerce. By analyzing customer behavior and preferences, ML algorithms enable businesses to anticipate needs and deliver value-added services. For example, an online retailer in Nigeria might use ML to offer personalized discounts to repeat customers or recommend complementary products based on past purchases. This level of customization fosters customer loyalty and drives sales, creating a win-win scenario for businesses and consumers alike.

In the context of sustainability, AI and ML are helping African businesses achieve their environmental, social, and governance (ESG) goals by optimizing resource utilization and reducing waste. Predictive analytics, for instance, can forecast demand with high accuracy, enabling businesses to produce only what is needed and minimize excess inventory. Similarly, AI-powered tools can monitor energy consumption across supply chain operations, identifying inefficiencies and suggesting corrective actions. In agriculture, precision farming technologies powered by ML are enabling farmers to use water, fertilizers, and pesticides more efficiently, reducing environmental impact while boosting yields.

One of the most transformative aspects of AI and ML in African supply chains is their potential to democratize access to advanced analytics. Historically, only large corporations with significant resources could afford sophisticated supply chain management tools. Today, cloud-based AI platforms and open-source ML frameworks are making these technologies accessible to small and medium-sized enterprises (SMEs), which form the backbone of Africa's economy. For example, an SME in Kenya can use a subscription-based AI tool to forecast demand, manage inventory, and optimize delivery routes without the need for substantial upfront investment. This democratization of technology is leveling the playing field and enabling SMEs to compete more effectively in local and international markets.

However, the successful implementation of AI and ML requires a robust data ecosystem. Data is the lifeblood of these technologies, and its quality and availability directly impact their effectiveness. In many African countries, the lack of standardized data collection and management practices poses a significant challenge. Businesses often rely on manual record-keeping or fragmented digital systems, resulting in incomplete or inaccurate data. Addressing this issue requires investments in digital infrastructure, such as data management platforms and analytics tools, as well as training programs to build data literacy among employees.

Another critical consideration is the ethical use of AI and ML in supply chains. These technologies have the potential to exacerbate existing inequalities if not implemented responsibly. For example, algorithmic bias can lead to unfair treatment of certain suppliers or customers, while excessive reliance on automation can displace workers in industries heavily dependent on manual labor. To mitigate these risks, businesses must adopt ethical AI principles that prioritize fairness, transparency, and accountability. Governments and industry associations can also play a role by establishing guidelines and standards for responsible AI use in supply chains.

Collaboration is key to unlocking the full potential of AI and ML in African supply chains. No single organization can address the continent's complex challenges alone. Partnerships between technology providers, governments, academic institutions, and non-governmental organizations (NGOs) are essential for driving innovation and scaling solutions. For instance, a public-private partnership that brings together an AI start-up, a logistics company, and a development agency could create a platform for optimizing last-mile delivery in remote areas, benefiting both businesses and communities.

The future of AI and ML in African supply chains is bright, with emerging trends pointing toward even greater innovation. One such trend is the integration of AI with other technologies, such as the Internet of Things (IoT) and blockchain. For example, combining IoT sensors with AI-powered analytics can provide real-time insights into the condition of goods, while blockchain ensures the integrity of this data. This convergence of technologies is creating more intelligent and secure supply chains, capable of adapting to dynamic market conditions and consumer demands.

Another promising development is the use of AI for supply chain scenario planning. Traditional methods of planning often rely on static models that fail to account for real-time changes and uncertainties. AI, however, can simulate multiple scenarios and recommend the best course of action based on a wide range of variables. For example, a logistics company anticipating a port closure due to extreme weather can use AI to evaluate alternative routes, assess the cost and time implications of each option, and implement the optimal solution. This level of agility is critical for navigating the complexities of African supply chains, where unpredictability is often the norm.

As African businesses continue to embrace AI and ML, the focus must shift from experimentation to scalability. Many organizations are already piloting AI projects, but the challenge lies in scaling these solutions across their operations and integrating them into existing workflows. This requires a clear strategy, strong leadership, and a commitment to continuous learning and improvement. By adopting a phased approach to AI implementation, businesses can gradually build their capabilities, gain stakeholder buy-in, and maximize the return on investment.

AI and ML represent a paradigm shift in how supply chains are managed, offering unprecedented opportunities for efficiency, innovation, and resilience. For Africa, these technologies are not just tools for optimization but catalysts for transformation, capable of addressing systemic challenges and unlocking new possibilities. As the continent continues to navigate its digital transformation journey, AI and ML will play an increasingly central role in shaping the future of supply chains, driving economic growth, and improving the quality of life for millions of people.

4.1 Enhancing Workforce Efficiency and Upskilling Through AI

While much of the focus on artificial intelligence (AI) and machine learning (ML) in supply chains revolves around operational optimization, their impact on workforce efficiency and skill development is equally significant. Automation driven by AI has the potential to alleviate employees from repetitive, low-value tasks, allowing them to focus on strategic and creative activities that add greater value to the supply chain. For example, instead of manually entering inventory data, employees can use AI-powered systems to automate these processes and dedicate their time to customer relationship management or supply chain strategy development.

In Africa, where supply chains often rely on labor-intensive processes, the integration of AI offers a path to increased productivity without necessarily reducing workforce size. Automation can complement human labor by handling monotonous or physically demanding tasks, such as data entry, quality control, and inventory sorting. For instance, in manufacturing facilities, AI-powered robotics can assist in assembling products or packaging goods, ensuring consistency and accuracy while allowing human workers to oversee the process and troubleshoot issues.

However, the adoption of AI and ML also highlights the urgent need for workforce upskilling. As supply chain operations become increasingly digital and data-driven, employees must acquire new technical skills to remain relevant and effective. Training programs that focus on data analysis, AI system management, and technology integration are essential for preparing the workforce for these changes. Companies must view upskilling not as an optional investment but as a strategic priority to ensure a seamless transition to AI-powered operations.

In sectors like logistics and warehousing, upskilling initiatives have already demonstrated success. For example, logistics providers have implemented training programs to teach drivers how to use AI-enabled route optimization tools, enhancing both their efficiency and job satisfaction. Similarly, warehouse employees are being trained to operate automated picking systems and collaborate with AI-driven machinery. These efforts not only improve operational outcomes but also foster a culture of innovation and adaptability within organizations.

Governments and educational institutions have a role to play in supporting workforce development through policies and programs that align with the needs of the AI-driven economy. Public-private partnerships can facilitate the creation of vocational training centers, certification programs, and apprenticeships that equip workers with the skills required for AI adoption in supply chains. For example, a partnership between a technology firm and a local university could develop a curriculum focused on AI in logistics, providing students with practical experience and job-ready skills.

4.2 AI's Role in Crisis Management and Resilience Building

One of the most compelling applications of AI in supply chains is its ability to enhance resilience and crisis management. Supply chains are increasingly exposed to disruptions caused by natural disasters, geopolitical tensions, and pandemics, and Africa's supply chains are particularly vulnerable due to infrastructure deficits and logistical challenges. AI-powered systems can help businesses anticipate, prepare for, and respond to these disruptions, minimizing their impact and ensuring continuity.

Predictive analytics, a core capability of AI, enables supply chain managers to identify potential risks before they materialize. By analyzing data from sources such as weather forecasts, geopolitical reports, and historical patterns, AI systems can provide early warnings about events that may disrupt supply chain operations. For instance, a logistics provider anticipating heavy rainfall in a particular region can reroute shipments or adjust schedules to avoid delays and damage to goods. This level of foresight is critical for maintaining operational efficiency in dynamic and uncertain environments.

During crises, AI plays a vital role in enabling rapid decision-making. Unlike traditional systems that rely on static models, AI-powered platforms can process real-time data and recommend actionable strategies. For example, during the COVID-19 pandemic, businesses that implemented AI-driven demand forecasting tools were better able to adapt to shifting consumer behavior, ensuring the availability of essential goods while avoiding overproduction of non-essential items. Similarly, AI-assisted supply chain visibility tools allowed companies to monitor the movement of goods and identify bottlenecks, enabling them to take corrective action promptly.

AI also contributes to post-crisis recovery by analyzing the impact of disruptions and recommending strategies for future resilience. For example, after a supply chain interruption caused by a natural disaster, AI systems can evaluate how the event affected production, transportation, and inventory levels, providing insights into how similar disruptions can be mitigated in the future. These insights are invaluable for long-term planning, helping businesses build more robust and adaptable supply chains.

Collaboration among stakeholders is essential for maximizing AI's potential in crisis management. Governments, businesses, and humanitarian organizations can leverage AI to coordinate responses to large-scale disruptions, such as food shortages or supply chain blockages. For instance, an AI-powered platform that integrates data from multiple stakeholders can identify areas with the greatest need for resources and optimize the distribution of aid. This collaborative approach ensures that resources are used efficiently and reach those who need them most.

Ethical considerations are particularly important in the context of AI-driven crisis management. Decisions made by AI systems must prioritize fairness and inclusivity, ensuring that vulnerable populations are not overlooked or disadvantaged. Transparency is also critical, as stakeholders must understand how AI-generated recommendations are formulated to build trust and accountability. Regulatory frameworks that promote responsible AI use in crisis scenarios are essential for addressing these ethical concerns and ensuring that AI serves the greater good.

5. Blockchain Technology in Supply Chain Visibility

Blockchain technology has emerged as a transformative force in supply chain management, offering a secure, transparent, and tamper-proof method for recording and verifying transactions. For Africa, where supply chains often struggle with inefficiencies, fraud, and a lack of trust, blockchain represents a powerful solution to address these challenges. By providing a decentralized ledger that all stakeholders can access and trust, blockchain enhances visibility, accountability, and efficiency in supply chain operations.

The essence of blockchain lies in its ability to create an immutable record of transactions. Each transaction is stored in a "block," which is then linked to the previous block, forming a continuous chain. This structure ensures that once a transaction is recorded, it cannot be altered or deleted without the consensus of all participants. This level of security and transparency is particularly valuable in African supply chains, where issues such as counterfeit goods, corruption, and inefficiencies are prevalent.

One of the most impactful applications of blockchain in African supply chains is in ensuring the authenticity and traceability of goods. For example, in the agriculture sector, blockchain can be used to track the journey of products from farm to table, ensuring that consumers receive high-quality, ethically sourced goods. A coffee producer in Ethiopia, for instance, can use blockchain to document the origin of their beans, the farming practices used, and the journey through the supply chain. This information can be accessed by buyers and consumers, building trust and enhancing the product's market value.

The mining industry, which plays a significant role in many African economies, also stands to benefit from blockchain technology. Issues such as illegal mining, conflict minerals, and environmental degradation have long plagued the sector. Blockchain can help address these issues by providing a transparent record of the mining process, from extraction to export. For instance, a diamond mining company can use blockchain to certify that its products are conflict-free and adhere to environmental and labor standards. This transparency not only enhances the company's reputation but also ensures compliance with international regulations.

Blockchain's potential extends to improving efficiency in customs and cross-border trade. Africa's supply chains often face delays and high costs due to complex customs procedures and inconsistent regulations. Blockchain can streamline these processes by providing a single, tamper-proof record of all necessary documentation, such as certificates of origin, invoices, and shipping manifests. For example, a logistics provider shipping goods from Kenya to Tanzania can use blockchain to share documentation with customs officials in real time, reducing delays and ensuring a smoother trade process.

The technology also plays a crucial role in combating fraud and corruption, which are significant challenges in African supply chains. By providing a transparent and verifiable record of transactions, blockchain eliminates opportunities for manipulation and ensures that all stakeholders are held accountable. For instance, a government procurement agency using blockchain can track every stage of the procurement process, from tendering to delivery, ensuring that funds are used as intended and reducing the risk of embezzlement.

In addition to enhancing transparency and accountability, blockchain can drive financial inclusion by enabling small-scale producers and traders to access formal markets and financial services. Many smallholders in Africa lack the documentation needed to establish trust with buyers or lenders, limiting their opportunities for growth. Blockchain can bridge this gap by providing a verifiable record of their transactions, production history, and compliance with standards. For example, a smallholder farmer in Ghana using blockchain to track their produce can demonstrate their reliability to buyers and secure better prices or access to credit.

Despite its potential, the adoption of blockchain in African supply chains faces several challenges. One of the primary barriers is the lack of digital infrastructure and reliable internet connectivity, particularly in rural areas. Blockchain systems require access to digital devices and networks, which may not be readily available to all stakeholders. Additionally, the cost of implementing blockchain solutions can be prohibitive for small and medium-sized enterprises (SMEs), which make up the majority of businesses in Africa.

Another significant challenge is the need for education and awareness. Many stakeholders in African supply chains are unfamiliar with blockchain technology and its benefits, leading to resistance or skepticism. Addressing this challenge requires targeted training programs and awareness campaigns that demystify blockchain and demonstrate its practical applications. Governments, industry associations, and technology providers must work together to build capacity and foster trust in the technology.

Regulatory frameworks are also critical for the successful implementation of blockchain in African supply chains. Governments must establish clear and supportive policies that enable the adoption of blockchain while ensuring compliance with international standards. For example, regulations that recognize blockchain-based records as legally binding can encourage businesses to adopt the technology and integrate it into their operations.

Collaboration among stakeholders is essential for maximizing the benefits of blockchain in supply chains. Public-private partnerships can provide the resources and expertise needed to implement blockchain solutions at scale. For instance, a partnership between a government agency, a technology company, and a logistics provider could develop a blockchain-based platform for tracking agricultural exports, benefiting farmers, traders, and regulators alike.

The role of blockchain in fostering trust and transparency cannot be overstated. In Africa, where fragmented supply chains and a lack of accountability often hinder growth, blockchain offers a transformative solution. By providing a secure, verifiable, and accessible record of transactions, the technology enables stakeholders to collaborate more effectively, reduce inefficiencies, and build resilient supply chains.

The future of blockchain in African supply chains is bright, with emerging trends pointing toward greater integration and innovation. For example, the convergence of blockchain with other technologies, such as the Internet of Things (IoT) and artificial intelligence (AI), is creating more intelligent and interconnected supply chain systems. IoT sensors can feed real-time data into blockchain networks, enhancing visibility, while AI algorithms can analyze blockchain data to optimize operations and predict trends.

As blockchain adoption grows, its impact will extend beyond individual supply chains to entire industries and economies. By enhancing transparency, reducing costs, and fostering trust, blockchain has the potential to transform African supply chains into engines of growth and development.

Small and medium enterprises (SMEs) form the backbone of Africa's economy, contributing significantly to employment and GDP. However, these businesses often face challenges such as limited access to markets, financing, and technology, which hinder their growth and integration into larger supply chains. Blockchain technology presents an opportunity to address these challenges by offering SMEs a transparent, secure, and scalable way to participate in formal supply chains.

For SMEs, one of the most significant advantages of blockchain is its ability to level the playing field. By using blockchain, small businesses can establish trust with buyers and suppliers without relying on traditional intermediaries. For example, an SME in Rwanda exporting handmade crafts can use blockchain to document the origin, production process, and quality of its products. This information not only builds trust with international buyers but also enhances the perceived value of the products, allowing the SME to compete in global markets.

Blockchain also facilitates access to financing for SMEs by creating a verifiable transaction history. Many small businesses struggle to secure loans or credit because they lack the documentation required to demonstrate their reliability. Blockchain addresses this issue by providing an immutable record of an SME's trading activity, including invoices, payments, and delivery records. Financial institutions can use this information to assess creditworthiness more accurately, enabling SMEs to access funding for expansion or operational needs.

Moreover, blockchain-based smart contracts can streamline transactions for SMEs, reducing administrative burdens and ensuring timely payments. Smart contracts are self-executing agreements with terms directly written into code, which automatically trigger actions when predefined conditions are met. For instance, a supplier using blockchain can receive payment automatically once a buyer confirms receipt of goods. This reduces the risk of payment delays and disputes, improving cash flow and operational efficiency for SMEs.

Counterfeiting is a major challenge in many African industries, from pharmaceuticals and electronics to luxury goods and agricultural products. The proliferation of counterfeit goods not only damages brand reputations but also poses significant risks to consumers. Blockchain technology offers a robust solution to this problem by providing an immutable record of product origin and movement through the supply chain.

In the pharmaceutical industry, blockchain can be used to ensure the authenticity of medicines and reduce the prevalence of counterfeit drugs, which are a significant public health concern in Africa. By assigning a unique digital identity to each batch of medicine and recording every transaction on a blockchain, manufacturers, distributors, and pharmacies can verify the authenticity of the product at every stage. For instance, a blockchain-based system can allow a pharmacy in Nigeria to scan a QR code on a medicine package and instantly access its production and distribution history, ensuring that it is genuine.

The agricultural sector also benefits from blockchain's ability to certify authenticity and quality. For example, a cocoa exporter in Côte d'Ivoire can use blockchain to document the journey of cocoa beans from farm to port, including details such as farming practices, certifications, and quality checks. This transparency not only enhances trust with buyers but also enables the exporter to charge premium prices for ethically sourced and high-quality products.

Blockchain's ability to combat counterfeiting extends to luxury goods and consumer electronics. By recording product details on a blockchain at the point of manufacture, companies can create a digital "passport" for each item that proves its authenticity. Consumers can access this information through a QR code or an app, ensuring that they are purchasing genuine products. This level of transparency enhances brand loyalty and protects consumers from fraudulent activities.

While blockchain holds immense potential, its scalability and interoperability remain significant challenges, particularly in the African context. Blockchain networks require substantial computational power and storage capacity, which can be resource-intensive and costly. For small businesses or organizations in regions with limited digital infrastructure, these requirements may pose barriers to adoption.

Interoperability is another critical issue, as different blockchain platforms often operate in silos, making it difficult for stakeholders to share information across networks. For example, a logistics company using one blockchain system may face challenges integrating its data with a retailer using a different platform. Addressing this issue requires the development of standardized protocols and frameworks that enable seamless data exchange between blockchain networks.

To overcome these challenges, industry stakeholders must collaborate on developing scalable and interoperable blockchain solutions. For instance, lightweight blockchain protocols designed for low-resource environments can make the technology more accessible to small businesses and rural communities. Additionally, governments and international organizations can support the development of shared blockchain infrastructure that serves multiple industries and stakeholders, reducing costs and fostering collaboration.

Another promising development is the use of tokenization in supply chains. Tokenization involves representing assets, such as goods or services, as digital tokens on a blockchain. These tokens can be traded or exchanged within the blockchain network, enabling more efficient and transparent transactions. For example, a logistics company transporting goods across Africa could use tokens to represent freight capacity, allowing stakeholders to book and pay for transportation services in a seamless and automated manner.

Blockchain is also expected to play a key role in advancing sustainability in supply chains. By providing verifiable records of environmental and social impacts, blockchain can help businesses meet growing demands for transparency and accountability in sustainability reporting. For instance, a fashion brand sourcing textiles from African suppliers can use blockchain to document compliance with fair labor practices and environmental standards, enhancing its reputation and market appeal.

5.1 Blockchain and Inclusive Trade Networks

Blockchain technology is creating opportunities to build more inclusive trade networks across Africa, bridging the gap between small-scale producers, informal traders, and larger formal markets. By providing a platform for decentralized and transparent transactions, blockchain enables marginalized groups to participate in supply chains on equal footing with larger players. This inclusivity is particularly valuable in Africa, where informal economies and smallholder farming dominate many sectors.

For example, small-scale fishers in Senegal could use blockchain to record and verify their daily catch, providing detailed data on the origin, quantity, and quality of their fish. This information, stored securely on the blockchain, would enable them to sell directly to wholesalers or exporters without relying on intermediaries, who often exploit these producers with unfair pricing. By cutting out middlemen, blockchain empowers small-scale producers to retain a larger share of the value they generate, boosting incomes and promoting local economic development.

Blockchain also facilitates cross-border trade among micro, small, and medium enterprises (MSMEs) by streamlining customs processes and reducing the administrative burden. For instance, an MSME in Uganda exporting handicrafts to Rwanda could use a blockchain-based platform to automate the submission of customs documentation, eliminating the need for lengthy manual procedures. This level of efficiency not only reduces costs but also enables faster access to new markets, fostering regional trade and economic integration.

Another benefit of blockchain for inclusive trade networks is its ability to provide a digital identity for businesses and individuals who lack formal documentation. Many small-scale producers in Africa do not have the records needed to establish their credibility with buyers or financial institutions. Blockchain solves this problem by creating a tamper-proof digital trail of their transactions, certifications, and compliance with industry standards. This digital identity serves as a trust-building mechanism, opening doors to new opportunities and partnerships.

5.2 Blockchain and Sustainable Supply Chains

Sustainability has become a central concern for businesses and consumers alike, and blockchain technology offers a powerful tool for creating more sustainable supply chains. By providing transparent and verifiable records, blockchain enables businesses to monitor and report on their environmental and social impacts, ensuring compliance with sustainability standards and enhancing accountability.

One area where blockchain is making a significant impact is in reducing deforestation and promoting sustainable land use. For instance, a timber company operating in the Congo Basin could use blockchain to track the origin of its wood and ensure it comes from certified sustainable sources. This data, accessible to regulators and consumers, helps combat illegal logging and supports the preservation of critical ecosystems.

Similarly, in the agricultural sector, blockchain can be used to promote sustainable farming practices. For example, a tea plantation in Kenya could document its use of organic farming methods and fair labor practices on a blockchain. This transparency builds trust with buyers and consumers, who increasingly demand products that align with ethical and environmental values. Additionally, blockchain enables traceability of carbon emissions along the supply chain, allowing businesses to identify hotspots and implement strategies to reduce their environmental footprint.

Blockchain also contributes to reducing waste and encouraging circular supply chains by providing visibility into the lifecycle of products and materials. In the electronics industry, for instance, blockchain can track the components of a device from manufacturing to disposal, facilitating recycling and reuse. This level of traceability supports the transition to a circular economy, where resources are conserved and waste is minimized.

Collaborative efforts among stakeholders are essential for scaling blockchain-based sustainability initiatives. Governments, NGOs, and industry associations can play a role in establishing standards and frameworks that guide the use of blockchain for sustainable supply chains. For example, a multi-stakeholder initiative could develop a blockchain-based certification program for African agricultural exports, ensuring compliance with international sustainability standards while enhancing market access.

6. Internet of Things (IoT) and Real-Time Monitoring in Supply Chains

The Internet of Things (IoT) is revolutionizing supply chain management by enabling real-time monitoring, predictive analytics, and automation. IoT refers to a network of interconnected devices equipped with sensors, software, and connectivity that allows them to collect and exchange data. In African supply chains, where inefficiencies and disruptions are common, IoT presents a game-changing opportunity to enhance visibility, optimize operations, and improve responsiveness.

The cornerstone of IoT in supply chains is its ability to provide real-time data on the location, condition, and movement of goods. By deploying IoT sensors on vehicles, shipping containers, and storage facilities, businesses can monitor the status of their assets throughout the supply chain. For instance, a logistics provider transporting fresh produce from Kenya to Uganda can use IoT sensors to track temperature and humidity levels in real time, ensuring that the goods remain fresh and meet quality standards. This level of visibility reduces losses and enhances customer satisfaction, which is particularly critical in industries like agriculture and pharmaceuticals.

IoT also plays a vital role in predictive maintenance, which minimizes downtime and extends the lifespan of critical assets. For example, IoT-enabled trucks used in cross-border transportation can send alerts when maintenance is needed, allowing fleet managers to address issues before they lead to breakdowns. This proactive approach not only reduces repair costs but also ensures timely deliveries, improving overall supply chain efficiency.

In warehousing, IoT is transforming operations by automating inventory management and streamlining workflows. IoT sensors can track stock levels in real time, eliminating the need for manual inventory checks and reducing the risk of stockouts or overstocking. For example, a warehouse in South Africa using IoT devices can automatically reorder supplies when inventory falls below a certain threshold, ensuring continuous availability of goods. Additionally, IoT-enabled robots can handle picking, packing, and sorting tasks, increasing productivity and accuracy in fulfillment operations.

IoT's impact extends to improving safety and security in supply chains. Theft and pilferage are common challenges in

African supply chains, particularly during transportation and storage. IoT-enabled tracking devices provide real-time location data, allowing businesses to monitor shipments and quickly respond to deviations or unauthorized activities. For example, a mining company transporting valuable minerals in Zambia can use IoT trackers to ensure the secure movement of goods and alert authorities in case of tampering or theft.

Another significant application of IoT in African supply chains is its role in reducing waste and promoting sustainability. By providing real-time insights into resource consumption, IoT enables businesses to identify inefficiencies and implement strategies to minimize waste. For instance, an IoT-enabled irrigation system used by farmers in Nigeria can monitor soil moisture levels and deliver precise amounts of water, reducing waste and conserving resources. Similarly, IoT sensors in warehouses can optimize energy usage by adjusting lighting and temperature based on occupancy and environmental conditions.

Despite its transformative potential, the adoption of IoT in African supply chains faces several challenges. One of the primary barriers is the lack of reliable internet connectivity and digital infrastructure, particularly in rural areas. IoT devices require constant connectivity to function effectively, and interruptions in network coverage can compromise their performance. Addressing this issue requires investments in broadband networks and alternative connectivity solutions, such as satellite or low-power wide-area networks (LPWANs), which are better suited for remote and underserved regions.

Another challenge is the cost of implementing IoT solutions, including hardware, software, and integration with existing systems. For many small and medium-sized enterprises (SMEs) in Africa, these costs can be prohibitive. Governments and development organizations can play a role in addressing this challenge by offering subsidies, grants, or low-interest loans to support IoT adoption. Additionally, technology providers can develop affordable, scalable IoT solutions tailored to the needs of African businesses.

Data security and privacy are critical concerns in IoT adoption. As IoT devices collect and transmit vast amounts of data, ensuring that this information is secure from cyber threats is essential. Businesses must implement robust cybersecurity measures, such as encryption, firewalls, and access controls, to protect their data and systems. Governments can also contribute by establishing regulations and standards for IoT security, ensuring that businesses adhere to best practices.

Education and capacity building are vital for unlocking the full potential of IoT in African supply chains. Many businesses lack the technical expertise needed to implement and manage IoT solutions effectively. Training programs and workshops can help supply chain professionals understand the benefits of IoT, learn how to use IoT tools, and troubleshoot common issues. Public-private partnerships can support these initiatives by pooling resources and expertise to deliver impactful training programs.

The future of IoT in African supply chains is bright, with emerging trends pointing toward even greater innovation. For example, the integration of IoT with blockchain technology is creating more transparent and secure supply chain systems. IoT sensors can feed real-time data into blockchain networks, ensuring that every transaction is verified and traceable. This combination of technologies is particularly valuable in industries where trust and accountability are critical, such as agriculture, mining, and healthcare.

Another exciting development is the use of IoT in autonomous transportation and delivery systems. Drones equipped with IoT sensors are already being used in countries like Rwanda to deliver medical supplies to remote areas, overcoming logistical challenges and saving lives. As drone technology becomes more advanced and affordable, its applications in supply chains are expected to expand, enabling faster and more efficient deliveries across Africa.

IoT's role in supply chain optimization also extends to smart cities, where interconnected systems enable seamless movement of goods and people. For example, IoT-enabled traffic management systems can optimize delivery routes, reducing congestion and improving efficiency in urban supply chains. Smart city initiatives in countries like South Africa and Kenya are laying the groundwork for integrating IoT into broader logistics ecosystems, creating more sustainable and resilient supply chains.

6.1 IoT and Last-Mile Delivery Optimization

Last-mile delivery is one of the most complex and cost-intensive components of supply chain management, especially in Africa, where infrastructure challenges, unstructured addresses, and remote locations often disrupt logistics. IoT technology offers innovative solutions to optimize last-mile delivery, improving efficiency and reducing costs while ensuring timely and accurate delivery to customers.

IoT-enabled GPS trackers and route optimization tools allow logistics companies to monitor delivery vehicles in real time, ensuring that drivers take the most efficient routes and avoid delays caused by traffic congestion or road closures. For example, a delivery company operating in Lagos, Nigeria, can use IoT systems to analyze traffic patterns and recommend alternative routes, ensuring that packages are delivered on time despite the city's notorious traffic jams.

Drones equipped with IoT sensors are also emerging as a game-changer for last-mile delivery in remote and underserved areas. In Rwanda and Ghana, drones are being used to deliver medical supplies, such as vaccines and blood, to rural communities that are difficult to access by road. IoT sensors on these drones monitor flight paths, weather conditions, and payload integrity, ensuring safe and efficient deliveries. As drone technology becomes more advanced and affordable, its use in e-commerce, agriculture, and humanitarian logistics is expected to expand across Africa.

Smart lockers and IoT-enabled parcel delivery systems are another innovation transforming last-mile logistics. These systems allow customers to retrieve packages from secure, automated lockers at their convenience, reducing the need for home deliveries. IoT sensors integrated into smart lockers monitor package status, ensuring that customers receive real-time updates on delivery progress. For instance, an e-commerce platform in South Africa could partner with local retailers to deploy IoT-enabled lockers in urban and suburban areas, providing a seamless and convenient delivery experience for customers.

One of the most powerful applications of IoT in supply chains is its ability to generate data for predictive analytics, enabling businesses to anticipate and mitigate risks. Supply chains are inherently vulnerable to disruptions, whether caused by natural disasters, equipment failures, or fluctuating market conditions. IoT technology enhances resilience by providing real-time insights and early warnings about potential issues.

For example, IoT sensors installed in storage facilities can monitor environmental conditions, such as temperature, humidity, and light exposure, ensuring that perishable goods are stored under optimal conditions. If sensors detect a deviation from the required parameters, they can send alerts to supply chain managers, enabling them to take immediate corrective action. This is particularly valuable in industries like agriculture and pharmaceuticals, where even minor deviations can result in significant losses.

IoT technology is also transforming fleet management by enhancing the safety and reliability of transportation assets. Sensors embedded in vehicles can monitor critical parameters such as engine performance, tire pressure, and fuel levels, providing fleet managers with actionable insights to prevent breakdowns. For instance, a logistics company transporting goods across East Africa could use IoT data to identify vehicles that require maintenance, reducing the risk of delays caused by mechanical failures.

Predictive analytics powered by IoT is equally valuable in addressing external risks, such as weather-related disruptions. By integrating IoT data with weather forecasts, businesses can predict the impact of adverse conditions on supply chain operations and develop contingency plans. For example, a shipping company anticipating heavy rainfall in West Africa could reroute shipments or adjust delivery schedules to minimize disruptions.

The full potential of IoT in supply chains is realized when it is integrated into collaborative ecosystems that bring together multiple stakeholders, including manufacturers, suppliers, logistics providers, and retailers. IoT enables seamless data exchange and real-time communication across these stakeholders, fostering greater transparency and coordination.

One example of an IoT-powered collaborative ecosystem is in the agricultural sector, where farmers, processors, and distributors work together to optimize supply chain efficiency. IoT sensors installed on farms can monitor soil conditions, weather patterns, and crop health, providing valuable data to processors and distributors about harvest timelines and yields. This data allows downstream stakeholders to plan logistics and inventory management more effectively, reducing waste and ensuring that products reach markets on time.

Another area where IoT fosters collaboration is in smart port operations. Ports are critical nodes in Africa's supply chains, and inefficiencies at ports can cause significant delays and costs. IoT technology is being used to create smart ports that enhance visibility and streamline operations. For example, IoT-enabled tracking systems can monitor the movement of shipping containers in real time, allowing port authorities, shipping companies, and customs officials to coordinate activities and reduce bottlenecks. Smart ports in countries like Kenya and South Africa are already demonstrating the benefits of IoT in improving throughput and efficiency.

IoT also facilitates collaboration in urban logistics, where multiple players are involved in managing last-mile deliveries. By integrating IoT data from delivery vehicles, traffic management systems, and customer apps, logistics companies can optimize delivery routes and schedules, ensuring that resources are used efficiently. For instance, a courier company operating in Nairobi could use IoT to coordinate deliveries with other companies, reducing congestion and minimizing environmental impact.

The integration of IoT with artificial intelligence (AI) and machine learning (ML) is also opening new possibilities for intelligent supply chain management. AI algorithms can analyze data collected by IoT devices to identify patterns, predict trends, and recommend actions. For example, an AI-powered platform using IoT data could predict demand fluctuations and automatically adjust production and inventory levels, ensuring optimal resource allocation.

As 5G networks become more widely available, the capabilities of IoT in supply chains will expand even further. The high-speed, low-latency connectivity provided by 5G enables the deployment of advanced IoT applications, such as autonomous vehicles and real-time video monitoring. For example, a logistics company using 5G-enabled IoT devices could deploy self-driving trucks to transport goods across Africa's highways, reducing labor costs and improving efficiency.

6.2 IoT and Cold Chain Logistics

Cold chain logistics, the transportation and storage of temperature-sensitive goods, is a critical component of supply chains in sectors such as agriculture, pharmaceuticals, and food processing. In Africa, maintaining cold chain integrity is particularly challenging due to unreliable infrastructure, frequent power outages, and logistical inefficiencies. IoT technology offers a transformative solution by enabling real-time monitoring and control of environmental conditions throughout the cold chain.

IoT-enabled sensors can monitor temperature, humidity, and light exposure inside storage units and transportation vehicles, ensuring that goods remain within prescribed conditions. For example, a pharmaceutical distributor transporting vaccines across Nigeria can use IoT sensors to track temperature fluctuations in real time. If a deviation occurs, the system can send alerts to supply chain managers, allowing them to take immediate corrective action, such as adjusting the refrigeration unit or rerouting the shipment.

In addition to monitoring, IoT systems can automate responses to environmental changes, further enhancing cold chain efficiency. Smart refrigeration units equipped with IoT technology can adjust settings dynamically based on sensor inputs, ensuring optimal conditions without manual intervention. For instance, a seafood exporter in Namibia could use IoT-enabled cold storage units that automatically adjust cooling levels during transit, preserving product quality and reducing spoilage.

IoT also improves visibility and traceability in the cold chain, which is essential for building trust with consumers and regulatory bodies. By integrating IoT data with blockchain technology, businesses can create an immutable record of a product's journey through the cold chain. A dairy producer in Kenya, for example, could document the temperature history of milk from farm to retail store, providing consumers with assurance about its freshness and quality. This transparency not only enhances brand reputation but also helps businesses comply with food safety regulations.

6.3 IoT and Workforce Empowerment

IoT technology is not only transforming supply chain operations but also empowering the workforce by improving efficiency, safety, and decision-making. In Africa, where supply chain operations often rely on manual labor, IoT provides tools that augment workers' capabilities and enable them to perform tasks more effectively.

For example, wearable IoT devices, such as smart helmets and wristbands, can enhance worker safety in warehouses and manufacturing facilities. These devices monitor environmental conditions, such as air quality and noise levels, and provide real-time alerts about potential hazards. In a warehouse in Ghana, workers equipped with IoT wearables could receive notifications about unsafe temperature levels or equipment malfunctions, allowing them to take precautionary measures and avoid accidents.

IoT also supports workforce productivity by automating routine tasks and providing actionable insights. Inventory management, which is traditionally labor-intensive, can be streamlined using IoT technology. Workers can use handheld IoT scanners to locate items in a warehouse quickly, reducing search times and improving order fulfillment rates. For instance, an e-commerce fulfillment center in South Africa could implement IoT-enabled inventory systems that guide workers to the exact location of products, minimizing errors and delays.

Training and skill development are critical for maximizing the benefits of IoT in the workforce. Many supply chain workers in Africa are unfamiliar with IoT technology and may require guidance on how to use it effectively. Companies can invest in training programs that teach workers how to operate IoT devices, interpret data, and troubleshoot common issues. For example, a logistics firm in Ethiopia could partner with a technology provider to deliver workshops on IoT applications, ensuring that employees are equipped to leverage the technology in their daily tasks.

IoT also enhances decision-making by providing workers with real-time data and insights. Field technicians, for instance, can use IoT devices to diagnose equipment issues remotely and determine the best course of action. A farmer in Tanzania using IoT-enabled irrigation systems could receive recommendations on water usage based on sensor data, optimizing crop yield while conserving resources. These applications not only improve operational outcomes but also empower workers to take ownership of their roles and contribute more effectively to supply chain success.

IoT is also expected to play a significant role in fostering urban logistics and smart city initiatives. As Africa's urban population grows, cities face increasing pressure to manage congestion, pollution, and resource consumption. IoT technology can address these challenges by enabling smarter traffic management, waste collection, and energy usage. For instance, IoT-enabled traffic sensors in Nairobi could optimize delivery routes, reducing congestion and improving air quality. Similarly, IoT-based waste management systems in Cape Town could monitor bin levels and schedule pickups dynamically, enhancing efficiency and sustainability.

7. The Rise of E-Commerce and Logistics Solutions in Africa

E-commerce has emerged as a transformative force in Africa, reshaping how businesses operate and consumers shop. The rapid growth of internet connectivity, mobile penetration, and digital payment solutions has created an ecosystem that supports the expansion of online retail. This shift has had a profound impact on supply chains across the continent, driving innovation, overcoming logistical barriers, and creating new opportunities for economic growth.

The rise of e-commerce in Africa is fueled by the continent's young and tech-savvy population, which is increasingly embracing online shopping. Platforms like Jumia, Konga, and Takealot have capitalized on this trend, offering consumers a convenient and diverse range of products at competitive prices.

These platforms rely heavily on digital technologies to manage supply chain operations, from inventory management and order processing to last-mile delivery. For example, Jumia uses advanced analytics and artificial intelligence (AI) to forecast demand, optimize inventory levels, and ensure that products are delivered on time.

Logistics plays a critical role in the success of e-commerce, and Africa's unique challenges have spurred the development of innovative solutions. One of the biggest obstacles to e-commerce growth is the lack of reliable addressing systems in many African countries, which makes it difficult to deliver goods to customers. To address this issue, logistics companies have developed digital addressing solutions, such as GPS-based systems and mobile apps, that enable precise location tracking. For instance, a customer in Nairobi can use a logistics app to share their exact location with a delivery driver, ensuring a seamless and efficient delivery experience.

Another challenge in African e-commerce is the cost and complexity of last-mile delivery, particularly in rural and remote areas. Logistics providers have responded by adopting creative solutions, such as motorcycle couriers, drones, and pickup points, to reach underserved regions. Drones, in particular, have shown great promise for e-commerce deliveries in Africa. Companies like Zipline have demonstrated the feasibility of using drones to deliver medical supplies, and similar models are being explored for e-commerce. By bypassing poor road networks and reducing delivery times, drones can significantly enhance the accessibility and reliability of e-commerce supply chains.

The rise of e-commerce has also spurred the development of shared logistics networks, where multiple retailers and logistics providers collaborate to optimize resource utilization. Shared warehousing, for example, allows e-commerce platforms to store products closer to customers, reducing delivery times and costs. In South Africa, shared logistics hubs in urban centers enable smaller e-commerce players to compete with larger platforms by providing access to advanced supply chain infrastructure at a fraction of the cost.

Technology is at the heart of e-commerce and logistics innovation in Africa, enabling businesses to address the continent's unique challenges. Digital payment solutions, such as mobile money platforms and e-wallets, have been instrumental in facilitating online transactions. In countries like Kenya and Ghana, mobile money services like M-Pesa and MoMo have made it possible for unbanked consumers to shop online, driving the adoption of e-commerce in previously untapped markets.

Artificial intelligence and machine learning are also playing a pivotal role in optimizing e-commerce supply chains. By analyzing customer data and purchasing patterns, AI-powered systems can forecast demand, recommend products, and personalize the shopping experience. For example, an e-commerce platform in Nigeria can use AI to identify trends in consumer behavior, ensuring that popular products are always in stock and that promotions are tailored to specific customer segments.

The integration of blockchain technology into e-commerce supply chains is another exciting development. Blockchain enhances transparency and traceability, addressing concerns about counterfeit goods and ensuring that products meet quality standards. For instance, an e-commerce platform selling organic produce can use blockchain to verify the origin and authenticity of its products, providing consumers with confidence in their purchases.

IoT is further transforming e-commerce logistics by enabling real-time tracking and monitoring of shipments. IoT-enabled devices installed on delivery vehicles and in warehouses provide data on the location, condition, and movement of goods, allowing businesses to optimize routes, prevent delays, and maintain product quality. For example, an e-commerce retailer in Egypt can use IoT sensors to monitor the temperature of perishable goods during transit, ensuring that they arrive fresh and in perfect condition.

The rise of e-commerce and logistics solutions in Africa is not just transforming supply chains; it is also driving significant socioeconomic change. By creating new jobs and empowering entrepreneurs, e-commerce is contributing to economic growth and reducing poverty. For example, online marketplaces like Jumia and Takealot provide a platform for small businesses and artisans to reach a broader audience, increasing their revenue and visibility.

E-commerce has also played a role in empowering women, who often face barriers to participating in traditional retail channels. Digital platforms provide female entrepreneurs with the flexibility to manage their businesses from home, enabling them to balance work and family responsibilities. For instance, a woman in Tanzania selling handmade jewelry can use an e-commerce platform to market her products internationally, overcoming the geographic and financial constraints of running a physical store.

The environmental impact of e-commerce is a growing concern, but technology offers solutions to minimize its footprint. For instance, shared logistics networks and route optimization tools reduce fuel consumption and emissions, making e-commerce supply chains more sustainable. Additionally, the adoption of electric delivery vehicles and eco-friendly packaging materials is helping e-commerce platforms reduce their environmental impact.

E-commerce also has the potential to bridge the urban-rural divide by connecting rural producers with urban consumers. Digital platforms that aggregate products from rural areas and deliver them to cities enable small-scale farmers and artisans to access larger markets. For example, an e-commerce company in Ethiopia could work with rural cooperatives to source organic coffee and distribute it to urban consumers, creating value for both producers and buyers.

Another promising trend is the rise of direct-to-consumer (DTC) brands, which bypass traditional retail channels to sell products directly to customers. DTC brands leverage digital tools to build strong relationships with their customers, offering personalized experiences and fostering loyalty. For instance, a skincare brand in South Africa could use a DTC model to offer customized products based on customer preferences and feedback, creating a more engaging and satisfying shopping experience.

Africa's e-commerce ecosystem is shaped by the continent's diverse consumer preferences, purchasing power, and access to technology. To thrive in this dynamic environment, e-commerce platforms must adapt their strategies to meet the specific needs of African consumers. One significant aspect is the prominence of mobile commerce (m-commerce), which has become the dominant mode of online shopping due to the widespread use of smartphones and mobile internet.

Mobile-optimized platforms are critical for capturing this market. For instance, an e-commerce app designed for Ghanaian consumers might prioritize features such as lightweight design for low-data usage and integration with mobile money platforms like M-Pesa or MoMo. These features cater to consumers who may lack access to traditional banking services or prefer mobile payments for convenience and security.

Another factor driving the adoption of e-commerce in Africa is the rise of social commerce, where businesses use social media platforms to engage with customers and sell products.

Social media channels like WhatsApp, Instagram, and Facebook are particularly effective in Africa, where they serve as both marketing tools and transaction platforms. For example, a small fashion retailer in Nigeria can use Instagram to showcase products, interact with customers, and process orders directly through the platform's messaging and payment features. This approach not only reduces operational costs but also builds stronger relationships with customers.

Trust remains a significant challenge in Africa's e-commerce landscape, as many consumers are wary of online transactions due to concerns about fraud and counterfeit products. E-commerce platforms are addressing this issue by implementing trust-building measures such as secure payment gateways, customer reviews, and robust return policies. For example, Jumia's pay-on-delivery option allows customers to inspect their purchases before making payment, reducing the perceived risk of online shopping. These measures are essential for fostering consumer confidence and encouraging repeat purchases.

Logistics is the backbone of e-commerce, and building resilient logistics networks is critical for the success of online retail in Africa. The continent's diverse geography and infrastructure challenges require innovative approaches to ensure that goods are delivered efficiently and cost-effectively.

One strategy is the use of distributed warehousing, where e-commerce platforms establish multiple small warehouses in strategic locations to reduce delivery times and costs. For example, an e-commerce company operating in East Africa might set up warehouses in Nairobi, Kampala, and Dar es Salaam, allowing it to serve customers in the region more quickly and efficiently. Distributed warehousing also enables platforms to manage inventory more effectively, ensuring that popular products are always in stock and accessible.

The adoption of multimodal transportation is another solution for overcoming logistical challenges in Africa. By combining road, rail, air, and sea transportation, e-commerce companies can navigate the continent's fragmented infrastructure and ensure reliable delivery. For instance, a retailer shipping products from South Africa to Botswana might use a combination of rail and road transport to optimize costs and transit times. Multimodal transportation not only enhances efficiency but also provides a contingency plan in case of disruptions to any single mode of transport.

Collaborative logistics networks, where multiple e-commerce players share resources, are also gaining traction in Africa. These networks enable smaller retailers to access advanced logistics infrastructure, such as shared warehouses and delivery fleets, without incurring prohibitive costs. For example, a group of online retailers in Lagos could pool resources to establish a shared logistics hub, allowing them to compete with larger platforms while reducing operational expenses.

The success of e-commerce depends not only on efficient logistics but also on providing a seamless and personalized customer experience. Technology plays a central role in achieving this goal, enabling e-commerce platforms to anticipate customer needs, address pain points, and build loyalty.

Artificial intelligence (AI) and machine learning (ML) are transforming how e-commerce platforms interact with customers. By analyzing browsing behavior, purchase history, and demographic data, AI-powered recommendation engines can suggest products tailored to individual preferences. For instance, an online bookstore in Kenya could use AI to recommend titles based on a customer's previous purchases, increasing the likelihood of repeat sales.

Personalization extends beyond product recommendations to include customized marketing campaigns and promotions. E-commerce platforms are leveraging data analytics to segment customers based on their preferences and behavior, allowing them to deliver targeted offers that resonate with specific groups. For example, a beauty retailer in South Africa might use analytics to identify customers interested in skincare products and send them personalized discount codes, driving engagement and sales.

Seamless payment options are another critical component of the customer experience. Many African consumers prefer flexible payment methods, such as pay-on-delivery or installment plans, which reduce the financial burden of large purchases. E-commerce platforms are increasingly offering these options, along with integration with digital wallets and mobile money services, to accommodate diverse consumer needs. For instance, a retailer in Tanzania could partner with a mobile money provider to enable customers to pay in installments, making products more accessible and boosting sales.

Sustainability is another area of focus for the future of e-commerce and logistics. As consumers become more environmentally conscious, e-commerce platforms are adopting eco-friendly practices to reduce their carbon footprint. This includes using electric delivery vehicles, biodegradable packaging, and optimized delivery routes to minimize emissions. For instance, an online grocery store in Kenya could use electric motorcycles for last-mile delivery, demonstrating its commitment to sustainability while enhancing its brand image.

The integration of advanced technologies, such as drones and autonomous vehicles, is also expected to drive innovation in e-commerce logistics. These technologies have the potential to reduce costs, improve delivery times, and reach underserved areas. For example, drones could be used to deliver small parcels to remote villages in Uganda, bypassing poor road infrastructure and ensuring timely deliveries.

7.1 Empowering Small Businesses Through E-Commerce Platforms

E-commerce has proven to be a powerful tool for empowering small businesses and entrepreneurs in Africa, providing them with access to broader markets and tools to compete with larger players. Many small and medium-sized enterprises (SMEs) face significant barriers to growth, including limited market reach, inadequate financing, and a lack of digital infrastructure. E-commerce platforms are addressing these challenges by offering affordable and scalable solutions tailored to the needs of small businesses.

Online marketplaces like Jumia, Konga, and Kilimall serve as virtual storefronts for thousands of SMEs, allowing them to showcase their products to a wide audience without the need for significant upfront investment. For example, a small-scale producer of handmade leather goods in Morocco can use an e-commerce platform to reach customers across the continent, overcoming the geographic limitations of traditional brick-and-mortar stores. This access to new markets not only increases sales but also enhances the visibility and competitiveness of small businesses.

E-commerce platforms also provide SMEs with tools and resources to improve their operations and customer engagement. Many platforms offer analytics dashboards that allow sellers to track sales, monitor customer behavior, and optimize their product offerings. For instance, a fashion retailer in Nigeria can use insights from an e-commerce platform to identify popular items and adjust inventory accordingly, reducing waste and maximizing profits.

Financing is another area where e-commerce platforms are making a difference for small businesses. By leveraging transaction data, e-commerce companies can assess the creditworthiness of sellers and provide access to working capital. For example, a digital lending program on an e-commerce platform could offer microloans to vendors based on their sales history, enabling them to invest in inventory or expand their operations. These financial services are particularly valuable for businesses that lack access to traditional banking systems.

The role of social media in empowering small businesses through e-commerce cannot be overstated. Social commerce, which combines social media and online shopping, has become a key channel for small businesses to engage with customers and build brand loyalty. Platforms like Instagram and Facebook enable entrepreneurs to create visually appealing content, interact with followers, and drive sales through direct messaging and integrated shopping features. For example, a jewelry designer in Kenya can use Instagram to showcase new designs, receive orders, and communicate with customers, creating a personalized shopping experience that fosters trust and loyalty.

7.2 Innovations in Returns Management and Reverse Logistics

Returns management and reverse logistics are critical components of e-commerce supply chains, yet they often pose significant challenges for businesses in Africa. High return rates, complex logistics, and inadequate infrastructure can result in increased costs and customer dissatisfaction. Innovations in technology and process optimization are helping e-commerce platforms address these challenges and create more efficient reverse logistics systems.

One of the key innovations in returns management is the use of data analytics and artificial intelligence (AI) to predict return trends and streamline processes. By analyzing customer behavior and historical data, e-commerce platforms can identify patterns in returns, such as specific products or regions with higher return rates. For example, an online retailer in South Africa might discover that a particular clothing brand has a higher return rate due to sizing issues. Armed with this insight, the retailer can provide more accurate sizing information or adjust the product description to reduce returns.

IoT technology is also playing a role in improving reverse logistics by enabling real-time tracking of returned items. IoT-enabled devices can monitor the condition and location of products as they are transported back to warehouses or sellers, ensuring that returns are processed quickly and efficiently. For instance, a logistics company handling returns for an e-commerce platform in Ghana could use IoT sensors to track shipments and provide updates to both the retailer and the customer, enhancing transparency and trust.

Shared logistics networks are another innovation in reverse logistics, allowing multiple e-commerce players to pool resources and optimize returns management. By collaborating on transportation and warehousing for returned items, businesses can reduce costs and improve efficiency. For example, a group of e-commerce platforms operating in East

Africa could establish a shared returns hub in Nairobi, where items are inspected, sorted, and redistributed, minimizing the environmental and financial impact of reverse logistics.

Sustainability is an increasingly important consideration in returns management. Many returned items end up in landfills due to the cost and complexity of restocking or refurbishing them. E-commerce platforms are adopting sustainable practices, such as refurbishing and reselling returned items, to reduce waste and promote circular supply chains. For example, an electronics retailer in Ethiopia might refurbish returned gadgets and sell them at discounted prices through a dedicated section on its website, creating value while minimizing environmental impact.

8. Data Analytics and Artificial Intelligence in Supply Chain Optimization

Data analytics and artificial intelligence (AI) are revolutionizing supply chains worldwide, and their adoption in Africa is unlocking new opportunities for efficiency, transparency, and resilience. In a region where supply chains often face challenges such as inefficiencies, high costs, and limited visibility, data-driven technologies are transforming decision-making and performance optimization. By harnessing the power of big data, predictive analytics, and AI, African businesses can overcome longstanding barriers and compete more effectively in global markets.

At the heart of supply chain optimization is the ability to collect, analyze, and act on data. Modern supply chains generate vast amounts of data from various sources, including sensors, transactions, customer interactions, and operational processes. Data analytics tools enable businesses to extract valuable insights from this information, helping them make informed decisions and respond proactively to changing conditions. For example, a logistics company in Kenya could use data analytics to monitor vehicle performance, optimize delivery routes, and reduce fuel consumption, resulting in significant cost savings.

AI takes data analytics to the next level by enabling machines to learn, adapt, and improve over time. Through machine learning algorithms, AI systems can identify patterns, predict trends, and recommend optimal courses of action. In supply chain management, AI is being used to forecast demand, optimize inventory levels, and enhance risk management. For instance, an AI-powered platform used by a retailer in South Africa could analyze historical sales data, weather patterns, and market trends to predict product demand during the holiday season, ensuring that inventory is stocked appropriately.

One of the most significant advantages of data analytics in supply chains is its ability to support real-time decision-making. Traditional supply chain processes often rely on static reports and historical data, which can lead to delays and suboptimal decisions. Real-time analytics, on the other hand, provides up-to-the-minute insights that enable businesses to respond quickly to dynamic conditions.

In the transportation sector, real-time data analytics is enhancing visibility and control over shipments. IoT devices installed on vehicles and shipping containers generate continuous streams of data, allowing logistics managers to track the location and condition of goods in real time. For example, a shipping company transporting goods from Egypt to Sudan could use real-time analytics to monitor traffic conditions, identify bottlenecks, and reroute vehicles to avoid delays. This level of agility is particularly valuable in Africa, where unpredictable infrastructure and road conditions often disrupt supply chain operations.

Real-time analytics also plays a crucial role in demand forecasting and inventory management. By analyzing data from sales channels, customer interactions, and market trends, businesses can adjust inventory levels dynamically to meet demand fluctuations. For instance, an online retailer in Nigeria could use real-time analytics to identify a sudden spike in demand for electronics during a promotional campaign, ensuring that warehouses are stocked and ready to fulfill orders promptly.

Supply chains are inherently vulnerable to disruptions, ranging from natural disasters and geopolitical conflicts to economic volatility and pandemics. AI-powered risk management tools are helping African businesses identify, assess, and mitigate these risks, enhancing resilience and continuity.

One of the key applications of AI in risk management is scenario planning. By simulating various scenarios and analyzing their potential impact, AI systems enable businesses to prepare for and respond to disruptions proactively. For example, a manufacturer in Ethiopia could use AI to model the impact of a raw material shortage on production timelines and identify alternative suppliers or materials to minimize delays.

AI is also transforming supplier risk assessment by analyzing vast amounts of data to evaluate supplier reliability, financial stability, and compliance with ethical standards. For instance, a retailer sourcing goods from multiple suppliers in Africa could use AI to rank suppliers based on performance metrics, such as on-time delivery rates and defect rates, ensuring that partnerships are established with trusted and dependable vendors.

Another critical area where AI enhances resilience is in detecting and mitigating fraud. Supply chains in Africa often face challenges related to corruption and counterfeit goods, which undermine trust and efficiency. AI-powered fraud detection systems analyze transaction patterns and flag anomalies, enabling businesses to identify fraudulent activities and take corrective action. For example, an agricultural exporter in Ghana could use AI to verify the authenticity of certifications and prevent fraudulent documentation from entering the supply chain.

Predictive analytics, a subset of data analytics, uses historical data and statistical algorithms to forecast future outcomes. This technology is particularly valuable in supply chain optimization, where accurate predictions can improve efficiency, reduce costs, and enhance customer satisfaction.

In logistics, predictive analytics is being used to anticipate delays and optimize delivery schedules. By analyzing factors such as weather conditions, traffic patterns, and shipment history, businesses can predict potential disruptions and adjust operations accordingly. For example, a logistics provider transporting goods across East Africa could use predictive analytics to identify high-risk routes during the rainy season and implement contingency plans to minimize delays.

Predictive analytics is also transforming inventory management by enabling businesses to maintain optimal stock levels. Overstocking ties up capital and increases storage costs, while understocking leads to lost sales and dissatisfied customers. Predictive analytics helps businesses strike the right balance by forecasting demand with high accuracy. For instance, a retailer in Tanzania could use predictive analytics to determine the optimal quantity of seasonal products to order, reducing waste and maximizing profitability.

In the manufacturing sector, predictive analytics is being used to enhance production planning and resource allocation. By analyzing data from production lines, equipment sensors, and market trends, manufacturers can optimize production schedules, reduce downtime, and improve overall efficiency. For example, a factory in Rwanda producing textiles could use predictive analytics to anticipate machine maintenance needs, ensuring continuous operation and preventing costly breakdowns.

While data analytics and AI offer immense potential, their adoption in African supply chains faces several challenges. One of the primary barriers is the lack of digital infrastructure and access to high-quality data. Many businesses still rely on manual record-keeping or fragmented digital systems, which limits their ability to harness the full power of analytics and AI. Addressing this challenge requires investments in data collection, storage, and processing infrastructure, as well as initiatives to improve data literacy among supply chain professionals.

Another challenge is the cost of implementing advanced analytics and AI solutions. Small and medium-sized enterprises (SMEs), which form the backbone of Africa's economy, often lack the resources to invest in these technologies. Governments and development organizations can play a role in addressing this issue by providing financial support, training programs, and incentives for technology adoption.

Despite these challenges, the opportunities presented by data-driven supply chains are vast. By embracing analytics and AI, African businesses can enhance efficiency, reduce costs, and improve competitiveness in global markets. Collaborative efforts among governments, private sector players, and technology providers will be critical for overcoming barriers and unlocking the full potential of these technologies.

One of the transformative impacts of data analytics in African supply chains is its ability to foster collaboration among stakeholders. Supply chains often involve multiple parties, including manufacturers, suppliers, logistics providers, retailers, and customers. Data analytics provides a unified platform for these stakeholders to share information, align goals, and coordinate actions, enhancing overall efficiency and transparency.

Collaborative platforms powered by data analytics allow stakeholders to gain real-time insights into supply chain operations. For instance, a manufacturer in Egypt could use a data-sharing portal to provide suppliers and logistics partners with visibility into production schedules, inventory levels, and shipping timelines. This shared visibility reduces misunderstandings, prevents delays, and ensures that all stakeholders work toward common objectives.

Demand planning and forecasting are also improved through collaborative analytics. By pooling data from various sources, businesses can develop more accurate demand forecasts and align their production and distribution strategies accordingly. For example, a retailer in Kenya could collaborate with suppliers and logistics providers to prepare for a major holiday season, using shared data to predict demand spikes and optimize inventory levels.

Collaboration through analytics also extends to risk management. By sharing risk data and insights, stakeholders can identify vulnerabilities and develop joint mitigation strategies. For example, a cross-border logistics company operating in West Africa could work with customs authorities, suppliers, and retailers to anticipate and address potential delays caused by regulatory changes or infrastructure disruptions. This level of coordination enhances supply chain resilience and minimizes the impact of unforeseen events.

As data analytics and artificial intelligence become integral to supply chain operations, ethical considerations must be addressed to ensure that these technologies are used responsibly and inclusively. In Africa, where data privacy regulations and digital literacy vary widely, businesses must navigate complex ethical challenges while leveraging data-driven technologies.

One critical ethical concern is data privacy and security. Supply chains generate and process vast amounts of sensitive information, including customer details, transaction records, and operational data. Protecting this data from breaches and unauthorized access is essential for maintaining trust among stakeholders. Businesses must implement robust cybersecurity measures, such as encryption, firewalls, and secure data storage systems, to safeguard information. For example, an e-commerce platform in South Africa could adopt end-to-end encryption to ensure that customer payment details remain secure during online transactions.

Transparency is another ethical consideration in data-driven supply chains. Stakeholders must understand how their data is being used and have the ability to opt out if they choose. Businesses should establish clear data governance policies and communicate them to all stakeholders, ensuring that data usage aligns with legal and ethical standards. For instance, a logistics company in Nigeria could create a transparency framework that outlines how data from IoT devices is collected, analyzed, and shared with partners.

Algorithmic bias is a growing concern in the use of AI for supply chain optimization. AI systems learn from historical data, which may contain biases that can influence decision-making. For example, an AI-powered supplier evaluation tool might favor large suppliers over smaller ones if historical data shows higher volumes from larger suppliers, even if smaller suppliers offer better quality or reliability. Businesses must regularly audit their AI systems to identify and address biases, ensuring that decisions are fair and inclusive.

Another ethical issue is the potential impact of automation on employment. As AI and automation become more prevalent in supply chains, there is a risk of job displacement for workers in roles that are automated. Businesses must balance the adoption of technology with efforts to reskill and upskill their workforce, enabling employees to transition into higher-value roles. For instance, a warehouse operator in Tanzania could provide training programs for workers to manage and maintain automated systems, ensuring that they remain relevant in an evolving supply chain landscape.

The integration of AI with blockchain technology is another exciting development. Blockchain provides a secure and transparent platform for recording supply chain transactions, while AI analyzes this data to generate actionable insights. For instance, an agricultural exporter in Ethiopia could use blockchain to verify the origin of its produce and AI to predict demand trends in international markets, ensuring optimal pricing and inventory management.

Another emerging application is the use of AI-powered autonomous systems in supply chain operations. Drones, self-driving trucks, and automated warehouses are becoming increasingly viable solutions for improving efficiency and reducing costs. For example, a logistics provider in Rwanda could deploy drones for last-mile deliveries in remote areas, while using AI algorithms to coordinate drone routes and schedules.

Sustainability will also play a central role in the future of data-driven supply chains. By analyzing environmental data, AI can help businesses reduce their carbon footprint and adopt more sustainable practices. For instance, a manufacturing company in South Africa could use AI to optimize energy usage on production lines, reducing emissions and lowering costs. Additionally, predictive analytics can support circular supply chain models by identifying opportunities for recycling, reuse, and resource recovery.

8.1 Democratizing Access to Data Analytics for Small and Medium Enterprises (SMEs)

One of the most significant barriers to adopting data analytics and artificial intelligence (AI) in African supply chains is the perception that these technologies are only accessible to large, well-funded corporations. However, democratizing access to these tools is critical for empowering small and medium enterprises (SMEs), which form the backbone of Africa's economy. By providing affordable, user-friendly, and scalable solutions, technology providers can help SMEs leverage data analytics to optimize their supply chain operations and remain competitive in the digital age.

Cloud-based data analytics platforms are a key enabler of democratization. These platforms allow SMEs to access powerful analytics tools without the need for significant upfront investment in infrastructure or software. For example, an SME in Uganda operating a small-scale manufacturing business could use a cloud-based analytics tool to track inventory levels, analyze sales patterns, and identify inefficiencies in production processes. With subscription-based pricing models, these platforms make advanced technologies accessible to businesses of all sizes.

Another approach to democratizing data analytics is through partnerships and collaborative programs. Governments, development organizations, and private sector players can collaborate to provide training, subsidies, and resources that enable SMEs to adopt analytics tools. For instance, a public-private partnership in Kenya could establish a digital training hub that equips SMEs with the skills and tools needed to integrate data analytics into their supply chain management. These initiatives not only level the playing field but also foster a culture of innovation and growth among small businesses.

Mobile-first analytics solutions are also gaining traction in Africa, where mobile penetration often exceeds access to traditional computing devices. Mobile apps that provide data visualization, real-time updates, and actionable insights enable SMEs to manage their supply chains on the go. For example, a mobile analytics app for a small agricultural cooperative in Tanzania could allow farmers to monitor market prices, track inventory, and coordinate logistics using their smartphones. By prioritizing mobile accessibility, technology providers can reach underserved communities and ensure that the benefits of data-driven supply chains are widely distributed.

8.2 Data Analytics for Sustainability and Environmental Impact

As sustainability becomes a global priority, data analytics is playing an increasingly important role in helping African supply chains minimize their environmental impact. By analyzing energy consumption, waste production, and resource usage, businesses can identify opportunities to reduce their carbon footprint and adopt more sustainable practices. In Africa, where environmental challenges such as deforestation, water scarcity, and pollution are pressing concerns, data-driven approaches to sustainability are particularly valuable.

One application of data analytics in sustainability is energy optimization. In industries such as manufacturing and logistics, energy consumption accounts for a significant portion of operational costs and environmental impact. Data analytics tools can monitor energy usage across facilities, identify inefficiencies, and recommend strategies for improvement. For instance, a textile manufacturer in Ethiopia could use analytics to optimize the operation of its machinery, reducing electricity consumption and lowering emissions.

Another area where data analytics is driving sustainability is in waste management and circular supply chains. By tracking material flows and analyzing production data, businesses can identify waste hotspots and implement measures to reduce, reuse, or recycle materials. For example, a food processing company in Ghana could use analytics to measure food waste at each stage of production and develop strategies to repurpose byproducts, such as converting organic waste into animal feed or bioenergy.

Logistics and transportation, which are significant contributors to greenhouse gas emissions, also benefit from data-driven sustainability initiatives. Route optimization tools powered by data analytics can minimize fuel consumption by identifying the most efficient delivery routes. For instance, a logistics provider in South Africa could use real-time traffic data and predictive analytics to reduce travel distances and idle time, contributing to lower emissions and operational costs.

Data analytics is also helping businesses meet sustainability reporting requirements and enhance transparency. Many global markets now demand detailed information about the environmental and social impacts of supply chain operations. Analytics platforms enable businesses to collect and report this data accurately, ensuring compliance with international standards and enhancing their reputation among environmentally conscious consumers. For example, a cocoa exporter in Côte d'Ivoire could use analytics to document its adherence to sustainable farming practices, building trust with buyers and consumers in global markets.

9. Automation and Robotics in Transforming African Supply Chains

Automation and robotics are revolutionizing supply chain operations globally, and Africa is beginning to embrace these technologies to address inefficiencies, reduce costs, and enhance productivity. In a continent where supply chains often face challenges such as labor shortages, infrastructure gaps, and high operational costs, automation and robotics offer a promising solution to bridge these gaps and drive transformation.

Automation refers to the use of technology to perform tasks with minimal human intervention, while robotics involves the use of programmable machines to execute physical tasks. Together, these technologies are reshaping supply chain functions, from manufacturing and warehousing to logistics and last-mile delivery. By reducing reliance on manual labor and improving operational accuracy, automation and robotics are enabling African businesses to compete more effectively in global markets.

One of the most significant applications of automation in African supply chains is in manufacturing. Automated production lines and robotic assembly systems are helping businesses increase output, reduce errors, and lower costs. For example, an automotive assembly plant in South Africa could use robotic arms to perform repetitive tasks, such as welding and painting, with greater precision and speed than human workers. This not only improves product quality but also enhances operational efficiency.

In warehousing, automation is transforming how goods are stored, retrieved, and packed for shipment. Automated storage and retrieval systems (ASRS) and robotic pickers are enabling warehouses to process orders faster and more accurately. For instance, an e-commerce fulfillment center in Nigeria could implement ASRS to store items in compact, high-density racks and deploy robotic arms to pick and pack orders. These systems maximize space utilization and reduce labor requirements, making them ideal for high-demand sectors like e-commerce and retail.

Last-mile delivery, the final leg of the supply chain, is one of the most challenging and cost-intensive aspects of logistics in Africa. Automation and robotics are providing innovative solutions to streamline last-mile delivery, particularly in urban and remote areas with infrastructure challenges.

Autonomous delivery vehicles, including drones and ground robots, are gaining traction as efficient and cost-effective alternatives to traditional delivery methods. Drones equipped with GPS and IoT sensors can navigate difficult terrain and bypass traffic congestion, ensuring timely deliveries. For example, a healthcare provider in Rwanda could use drones to deliver medical supplies to remote villages, reducing delivery times and saving lives. Similarly, autonomous ground robots can navigate urban environments to deliver packages directly to customers' doorsteps, offering a convenient and reliable service.

In addition to improving delivery efficiency, autonomous vehicles reduce operational costs by eliminating the need for drivers and minimizing fuel consumption. This makes them particularly valuable for businesses operating in regions where labor and fuel costs are high. However, the adoption of autonomous vehicles in Africa faces challenges such as regulatory barriers, infrastructure limitations, and public acceptance. Addressing these challenges requires collaboration among governments, technology providers, and logistics companies to create an enabling environment for innovation.

Collaborative robots, or cobots, are designed to work alongside human workers, enhancing productivity and safety in supply chain operations. Unlike traditional industrial robots, which are typically confined to specific tasks, cobots are flexible and adaptable, making them ideal for dynamic environments like warehouses and production lines.

In warehousing, cobots can assist workers with tasks such as sorting, packing, and transporting goods. For instance, a logistics company in Kenya could deploy cobots to help employees move heavy items, reducing physical strain and improving workplace safety. Cobots can also be programmed to learn new tasks, allowing businesses to adapt quickly to changing operational requirements.

In manufacturing, cobots are being used to automate repetitive and labor-intensive processes, enabling workers to focus on more complex and creative tasks. For example, a garment factory in Ethiopia could use cobots to sew fabric and assemble garments, while workers handle quality control and design adjustments. This division of labor enhances efficiency and allows businesses to scale production without increasing workforce size.

Cobots are also more affordable and easier to integrate than traditional industrial robots, making them accessible to small and medium-sized enterprises (SMEs). By adopting cobots, African businesses can modernize their operations without incurring prohibitive costs, driving innovation and competitiveness across industries.

While automation and robotics hold immense potential for transforming African supply chains, their adoption faces several challenges. One of the primary barriers is the high upfront cost of acquiring and implementing these technologies. For many businesses, particularly SMEs, the initial investment required for automation and robotics systems can be prohibitive. Governments and development organizations can address this issue by offering subsidies, grants, or financing programs that support technology adoption.

Another challenge is the lack of technical expertise needed to operate and maintain automation and robotics systems. Many African businesses struggle to find skilled professionals who can manage these technologies effectively. Investing in education and training programs is essential to building a workforce capable of supporting the transition to automated supply chains. For example, a vocational training center in Ghana could offer courses in robotics programming, maintenance, and troubleshooting, equipping workers with the skills needed for the future of supply chain management.

Infrastructure limitations also pose a challenge to automation adoption, particularly in rural and underserved areas. Reliable electricity, internet connectivity, and transportation networks are critical for the successful deployment of automated systems. Governments and private sector players must prioritize infrastructure development to create an environment conducive to technological innovation.

Despite these challenges, the opportunities presented by automation and robotics are vast. By improving efficiency, reducing costs, and enhancing resilience, these technologies can help African businesses overcome supply chain challenges and unlock new levels of growth and competitiveness. Additionally, the adoption of automation and robotics aligns with global trends toward digital transformation, positioning African businesses as key players in the global economy.

Agriculture remains the backbone of many African economies, accounting for a significant portion of employment and GDP. However, the sector faces challenges such as labor shortages, low productivity, and post-harvest losses. Robotics is emerging as a transformative solution, automating key agricultural processes and enabling farmers to achieve greater efficiency and yield.

One application of robotics in African agriculture is in planting and harvesting. Autonomous tractors and robotic harvesters equipped with GPS and sensors can perform tasks such as sowing seeds, applying fertilizers, and picking crops with precision and speed. For instance, a large-scale farm in Kenya could deploy autonomous tractors to plow fields and plant maize, reducing labor requirements and ensuring uniform crop growth. Robotic harvesters can also minimize losses by carefully handling produce, particularly for delicate crops like fruits and vegetables.

Drones are another innovative tool being used in African agriculture. Equipped with cameras and sensors, drones can monitor crop health, detect pests and diseases, and assess irrigation needs. For example, a tea plantation in Rwanda could use drones to scan fields for signs of pest infestations, allowing farmers to take targeted action before significant damage occurs. By providing real-time data on crop conditions, drones enable farmers to make informed decisions and optimize resource usage.

Post-harvest automation is also addressing one of the most critical challenges in African agriculture—post-harvest losses. Robotic sorting and grading systems can process harvested crops quickly and accurately, ensuring that only high-quality produce reaches markets. For instance, a mango exporter in Côte d'Ivoire could use robotic graders to sort mangoes by size, weight, and ripeness, enhancing product quality and increasing market value.

While automation and robotics offer immense benefits, their adoption in African supply chains raises important ethical and socioeconomic considerations. One of the most significant concerns is the potential impact on employment. Automation can displace workers in roles that are traditionally labor-intensive, particularly in sectors like manufacturing, logistics, and agriculture. Addressing this challenge requires a balanced approach that prioritizes workforce reskilling and job creation in new technology-driven roles.

For instance, governments and businesses can invest in training programs that equip workers with skills in robotics programming, maintenance, and operation. A vocational training center in South Africa, for example, could offer courses that prepare displaced factory workers for roles in managing and troubleshooting automated systems. By providing opportunities for reskilling, businesses can ensure that workers remain active participants in the evolving supply chain landscape.

Another ethical consideration is the accessibility of automation technologies. High costs often limit their adoption to large corporations, leaving small and medium-sized enterprises (SMEs) at a disadvantage. To promote inclusivity, technology providers can develop affordable and scalable automation solutions tailored to the needs of SMEs. Governments and development organizations can also play a role by offering subsidies or incentives to support technology adoption among smaller businesses.

The environmental impact of automation and robotics is another important consideration. While these technologies can enhance efficiency and reduce resource consumption, they also require energy to operate and often rely on materials that are difficult to recycle. Businesses must adopt sustainable practices, such as using energy-efficient robotics and exploring circular supply chain models that prioritize recycling and reuse.

Collaboration among stakeholders is critical for addressing these ethical and socioeconomic challenges. Governments, industry associations, and technology providers must work together to establish guidelines and frameworks that promote responsible automation adoption. For instance, a multi-stakeholder initiative in Nigeria could develop a national strategy for automation that balances technological advancement with job creation and environmental sustainability.

Public-private partnerships (PPPs) are playing an increasingly important role in advancing automation and robotics in African supply chains. By pooling resources, expertise, and funding, PPPs can accelerate the development and deployment of automation technologies across industries.

One example of a successful PPP is the establishment of innovation hubs that foster research and development (R&D) in robotics and automation. These hubs bring together government agencies, academic institutions, and private sector players to create an ecosystem that supports technological innovation. For instance, an innovation hub in Ethiopia focused on agricultural robotics could develop cost-effective solutions for smallholder farmers, such as autonomous irrigation systems or robotic weeders.

PPPs are also driving infrastructure development, which is essential for supporting automation adoption. Governments can partner with technology providers and logistics companies to build the physical and digital infrastructure needed for automated supply chains, such as high-speed internet, electricity grids, and advanced logistics hubs. For example, a PPP in Ghana could develop a network of smart warehouses equipped with automated storage and retrieval systems, enhancing supply chain efficiency and competitiveness.

Another area where PPPs are making an impact is in capacity building and education. By funding training programs and scholarships, PPPs can ensure that the workforce is prepared for the demands of an automated economy. For instance, a partnership between a robotics company and a university in Kenya could establish a robotics training center, providing students with hands-on experience and industry-relevant skills.

9.1 Automation in Customization and Personalized Manufacturing

The advent of automation and robotics is not only revolutionizing mass production but also enabling customization and personalized manufacturing. In Africa, where diverse consumer preferences and cultural nuances play a significant role in purchasing decisions, automation is helping businesses tailor products to meet individual and regional demands. This shift from mass production to mass customization is particularly valuable in industries such as fashion, consumer electronics, and food processing.

One application of automation in personalized manufacturing is the use of robotic systems to produce customized products on demand. For example, a fashion retailer in Nigeria could use automated sewing machines and robotic cutters to create made-to-measure garments based on customer specifications. By integrating automation with digital design tools, businesses can streamline the production process, reduce waste, and deliver high-quality products tailored to individual needs.

Additive manufacturing, commonly known as 3D printing, is another transformative technology enabling customization. With 3D printers, businesses can produce complex and unique items without the need for extensive tooling or assembly lines. For instance, a small-scale jewelry maker in Kenya could use 3D printing to create intricate designs that cater to local tastes and preferences, enhancing competitiveness and customer satisfaction. The ability to produce on demand also reduces inventory costs and minimizes the risk of overproduction.

Automation is also playing a role in personalized food production, where robotic systems can prepare meals or process ingredients based on individual dietary requirements. For example, a food processing company in South Africa could use automated systems to produce gluten-free or vegan snacks, addressing the growing demand for specialized products. This level of customization not only meets consumer expectations but also opens new market opportunities for businesses willing to invest in automation technologies.

9.2 Robotics for Hazardous and High-Risk Tasks

Another critical area where robotics is making an impact in African supply chains is in performing hazardous and high-risk tasks. These include activities that are dangerous, labor-intensive, or require a high level of precision, where human workers are at risk of injury or errors. By deploying robots in such scenarios, businesses can enhance safety, reduce accidents, and maintain operational efficiency.

In the mining sector, which is a cornerstone of many African economies, robotics is being used to improve safety and productivity. Autonomous mining vehicles, robotic drills, and remote-operated machinery are reducing the need for workers to operate in hazardous underground environments. For example, a gold mining operation in Ghana could deploy robotic loaders to transport ore from deep mines, minimizing the risk of cave-ins and exposure to toxic gases.

Robots are also transforming hazardous tasks in the chemical and pharmaceutical industries, where handling volatile substances requires precision and care. Robotic arms equipped with advanced sensors can mix, measure, and package chemicals without direct human intervention, ensuring accuracy and reducing the risk of spills or contamination. For instance, a pharmaceutical manufacturer in Egypt could use robots to prepare and package medications in sterile environments, maintaining high standards of safety and quality.

The energy sector is another area where robotics is addressing high-risk tasks. Robotic systems are being used to inspect and maintain infrastructure, such as pipelines, power lines, and wind turbines. For example, drones equipped with cameras and thermal sensors can inspect oil pipelines in Nigeria for leaks or damage, reducing the need for manual inspections in remote or dangerous locations. Similarly, robots designed for underwater operations can inspect offshore oil rigs, ensuring the safety and integrity of critical infrastructure.

9.3 The Intersection of Robotics and Artificial Intelligence in African Supply Chains

The integration of robotics with artificial intelligence (AI) is unlocking new possibilities for supply chain optimization in Africa. AI-powered robots can learn from data, adapt to new tasks, and make decisions in real time, making them ideal for dynamic and complex supply chain environments.

One of the most significant applications of AI-driven robotics is in predictive maintenance. By analyzing data from sensors embedded in robots and other equipment, AI systems can predict when maintenance is needed, preventing unexpected breakdowns and reducing downtime. For example, a logistics company in Kenya could use AI-powered robotics to monitor the condition of automated conveyor belts in a warehouse, ensuring that maintenance is performed proactively.

AI is also enhancing the decision-making capabilities of robots, enabling them to operate autonomously in unpredictable environments. In last-mile delivery, for instance, autonomous delivery robots equipped with AI can navigate urban areas, avoid obstacles, and adjust routes based on traffic conditions. For example, an e-commerce platform in South Africa could deploy AI-powered delivery robots to transport packages to customers' homes, offering a seamless and reliable delivery experience.

In addition to operational efficiency, the combination of AI and robotics is driving innovation in product development. AI algorithms can analyze consumer data to identify trends and preferences, which robots can then use to produce customized products. For example, a home appliance manufacturer in Morocco could use AI to identify popular features among consumers and program robots to assemble products that meet these specifications.

10. Sustainability in African Supply Chains

Sustainability has become a critical priority in global supply chains, and Africa is no exception. As environmental concerns, social equity, and ethical considerations take center stage, businesses across the continent are increasingly adopting strategies to make their supply chains greener, more inclusive, and more resilient. For Africa, where natural resources are abundant but often mismanaged, sustainable supply chain practices offer a path to long-term economic growth and environmental preservation.

Sustainability in supply chains encompasses three main pillars: environmental, social, and economic. The environmental pillar focuses on reducing carbon emissions, minimizing waste, and conserving natural resources. The social pillar emphasizes fair labor practices, community engagement, and social equity. The economic pillar aims to ensure profitability and competitiveness while fostering inclusive growth. In Africa, integrating these pillars into supply chain operations is both a challenge and an opportunity, requiring collaboration among governments, businesses, and communities.

One of the most significant challenges in African supply chains is the high level of carbon emissions associated with transportation, manufacturing, and energy use. Businesses are adopting strategies to reduce their carbon footprint by optimizing logistics, transitioning to renewable energy sources, and implementing energy-efficient technologies. For example, a logistics company operating in East Africa could use route optimization software to minimize fuel consumption and emissions, reducing both costs and environmental impact.

Renewable energy is playing an increasingly important role in powering supply chain operations. Solar panels, wind turbines, and hydropower are being used to provide clean and reliable energy for warehouses, factories, and transportation systems. For instance, a manufacturing plant in South Africa could install solar panels to power production lines, cutting energy costs and reducing reliance on fossil fuels. These investments not only enhance sustainability but also improve resilience against power outages, which are common in many parts of Africa.

Circular supply chains are emerging as a solution to waste management challenges, focusing on recycling, reusing, and repurposing materials to extend their lifecycle. In industries such as fashion, electronics, and agriculture, businesses are adopting circular practices to reduce waste and create value from byproducts.

For example, a clothing retailer in Nigeria could collect used garments from customers and recycle them into new fabrics or products, reducing textile waste and conserving resources. Similarly, an electronics manufacturer in Kenya could establish a take-back program for old devices, recovering valuable materials such as metals and plastics for reuse in production. These circular practices not only reduce environmental impact but also foster innovation and competitiveness in resource-constrained markets.

In agriculture, circular supply chains are addressing food waste by repurposing byproducts into valuable inputs. For instance, a sugarcane processor in Uganda could convert bagasse (the fibrous residue left after extracting juice) into bioenergy or animal feed, reducing waste and generating additional revenue streams. These practices contribute to sustainable agriculture while supporting rural livelihoods and economic growth.

Social sustainability is a critical aspect of supply chain management, focusing on the well-being of workers and communities involved in production and distribution. In Africa, where informal labor and exploitative practices are prevalent, businesses are taking steps to ensure fair wages, safe working conditions, and equitable opportunities.

For example, a cocoa exporter in Côte d'Ivoire could partner with farmer cooperatives to provide training, fair pricing, and access to markets, improving livelihoods and promoting ethical sourcing. Certifications such as Fair Trade and Rainforest Alliance are also helping businesses demonstrate their commitment to social sustainability, building trust with consumers and stakeholders.

Worker welfare initiatives extend beyond wages to include access to healthcare, education, and skill development. A logistics company in Ghana, for instance, could establish a worker training program to enhance productivity and career advancement, while providing health insurance and childcare support for employees. These investments not only improve employee satisfaction but also enhance operational efficiency and brand reputation.

Sustainable supply chains play a vital role in supporting local economies and small and medium-sized enterprises (SMEs). By sourcing locally, businesses reduce transportation costs, minimize carbon emissions, and foster economic inclusion. For instance, a food processing company in Kenya could source raw materials from local farmers, creating a reliable market for agricultural produce while reducing its environmental footprint.

SMEs are also benefiting from technology-driven platforms that connect them to larger supply chains. E-commerce and digital marketplaces are providing small businesses with access to broader markets, enabling them to compete on a global scale.

For example, an artisan in Tanzania could use an online platform to sell handmade crafts to international buyers, enhancing income and visibility.

While the benefits of sustainability in African supply chains are clear, the journey is not without challenges. Limited access to resources, inadequate infrastructure, and regulatory barriers often hinder the adoption of sustainable practices. Addressing these challenges requires collaboration and innovation at multiple levels.

One key challenge is the high cost of implementing sustainable technologies, such as renewable energy systems and waste management infrastructure. Governments and development organizations can support businesses by offering incentives, grants, and subsidies for sustainable investments. For instance, a government program in Ethiopia could provide tax breaks for companies that adopt energy-efficient technologies, encouraging widespread adoption.

Another challenge is the lack of awareness and expertise in sustainable supply chain management. Training programs, workshops, and educational campaigns are essential for building capacity and fostering a culture of sustainability. For example, a partnership between a university and an industry association in South Africa could develop a certification program in sustainable logistics, equipping professionals with the skills needed to drive change.

Regulatory frameworks also play a critical role in promoting sustainability. Governments must establish clear and enforceable policies that incentivize sustainable practices and hold businesses accountable for environmental and social impacts. For example, a policy requiring companies to disclose their carbon emissions could encourage transparency and drive innovation in emission reduction strategies.

The adoption of technology is playing a transformative role in advancing sustainability in African supply chains. Digital tools and innovative solutions are enabling businesses to monitor, measure, and optimize their environmental and social impacts. By leveraging technologies such as blockchain, the Internet of Things (IoT), and artificial intelligence (AI), companies can enhance transparency, accountability, and efficiency, paving the way for greener and more ethical operations.

Blockchain technology is revolutionizing supply chain transparency by providing an immutable and decentralized record of transactions. In industries such as agriculture, mining, and fashion, blockchain enables businesses to trace the origin of raw materials and verify compliance with sustainability standards. For instance, a coffee exporter in Ethiopia could use blockchain to document the journey of coffee beans from farm to cup, ensuring that they are ethically sourced and produced under fair labor conditions. This level of traceability builds trust with consumers and enhances the exporter's reputation in global markets.

Blockchain is also helping businesses address issues such as counterfeit goods and corruption. By providing a verifiable record of transactions, blockchain ensures that products meet quality standards and regulatory requirements. For example, a pharmaceutical company in Nigeria could use blockchain to verify the authenticity of medicines and prevent the circulation of counterfeit drugs, protecting both consumers and public health.

The Internet of Things (IoT) is another game-changing technology driving sustainability in African supply chains. IoT devices equipped with sensors can monitor resource usage, environmental conditions, and equipment performance in real time, enabling businesses to optimize operations and reduce waste. For example, a cold storage facility in Kenya could use IoT sensors to monitor temperature and energy consumption, ensuring that perishable goods are stored efficiently while minimizing electricity usage.

IoT is also transforming waste management by providing data on material flows and enabling predictive maintenance. A manufacturing plant in South Africa, for instance, could use IoT sensors to track waste generation at each stage of production and identify opportunities for recycling or reuse. Similarly, IoT-enabled machinery can detect signs of wear and tear, allowing businesses to perform maintenance proactively and avoid costly breakdowns.

Artificial intelligence (AI) is enhancing sustainability by providing businesses with predictive insights and actionable recommendations. AI-powered systems can analyze large datasets to identify inefficiencies, forecast demand, and optimize resource allocation. For example, an agricultural cooperative in Ghana could use AI to predict crop yields and plan resource usage, ensuring that water, fertilizers, and pesticides are used efficiently.

AI is also helping businesses assess their environmental impact and develop strategies for improvement. A logistics company in Tanzania, for instance, could use AI to analyze its carbon footprint and recommend measures to reduce emissions, such as adopting electric vehicles or optimizing delivery routes. By integrating AI into their operations, businesses can achieve greater sustainability while maintaining profitability.

Women play a vital role in African supply chains, particularly in agriculture and small-scale manufacturing. However, they often face barriers such as limited access to resources, markets, and decision-making power. Sustainable supply chain initiatives are addressing these challenges by providing women with training, financing, and market access.

For instance, a shea butter cooperative in Burkina Faso could partner with a global cosmetics brand to source raw materials ethically while empowering female producers. By providing fair wages, capacity-building programs, and infrastructure support, the partnership ensures that women benefit economically and socially from their participation in the supply chain.

Smallholder farmers are at the heart of African agriculture, yet they often struggle with low productivity, market access, and vulnerability to climate change. Sustainable supply chain practices are helping farmers overcome these challenges by integrating them into formal markets and providing them with resources and support.

For example, a food processing company in Uganda could work with smallholder maize farmers to improve productivity and reduce post-harvest losses. Through training programs, access to improved seeds, and partnerships with logistics providers, the company ensures a steady supply of quality raw materials while improving farmers' incomes and livelihoods.

Africa's growing youth population represents a significant opportunity for supply chain innovation and sustainability. By engaging young people in sustainable supply chain initiatives, businesses can drive innovation, address labor shortages, and promote economic inclusion. For instance, a renewable energy company in Kenya could train young entrepreneurs to install and maintain solar-powered cold storage systems for rural farmers, creating jobs and enhancing food security.

Infrastructure deficits, such as inadequate transportation networks and unreliable power supply, remain significant barriers to sustainability in Africa. To address these challenges, businesses and governments are investing in resilient and sustainable infrastructure. For example, a government-led initiative in Rwanda could develop a network of green logistics hubs powered by renewable energy, enhancing supply chain efficiency and reducing emissions.

Achieving sustainability requires a shift in mindset among businesses, consumers, and policymakers. Educational campaigns and awareness programs are critical for driving behavior change and fostering a culture of sustainability. For instance, a public awareness campaign in Nigeria could highlight the benefits of recycling and encourage consumers to participate in circular supply chains by returning used products for recycling or refurbishment.

10.1 Promoting Sustainable Packaging and Waste Reduction

Packaging is an integral part of supply chains, but its environmental impact is significant, particularly in regions with limited waste management infrastructure. Sustainable packaging practices are emerging as a critical focus for African businesses seeking to reduce their environmental footprint while meeting consumer demands for eco-friendly products.

Many African companies are replacing conventional plastic packaging with biodegradable or reusable materials to minimize waste. For instance, a beverage manufacturer in Ghana might adopt plant-based bottles or compostable packaging for its products, reducing plastic pollution and appealing to environmentally conscious consumers. Similarly, retailers are encouraging the use of reusable shopping bags instead of single-use plastics, fostering a culture of sustainability among customers.

Start-ups and social enterprises are also driving innovation in sustainable packaging. For example, a Kenyan start-up might produce packaging materials from agricultural waste, such as sugarcane fibers or banana leaves, creating eco-friendly alternatives while supporting local farmers. These innovations not only reduce waste but also create new economic opportunities in rural areas.

Circular packaging systems are another strategy for reducing waste in African supply chains. Businesses are adopting models where packaging materials are collected, cleaned, and reused, creating a closed-loop system that minimizes waste and conserves resources. For example, a cosmetics company in South Africa could introduce a refill program, allowing customers to return empty containers for refills at a discounted price. This approach reduces packaging waste while building customer loyalty.

Digital tools are also facilitating the transition to circular packaging systems. IoT-enabled tracking systems, for instance, can monitor the lifecycle of packaging materials, ensuring that they are recovered and reused efficiently. A logistics company in Nigeria could use IoT to track the movement of reusable pallets and crates, optimizing their collection and redistribution to reduce waste and transportation costs.

10.2 Community Engagement in Sustainable Supply Chains

Sustainability is most effective when it involves the active participation of communities. By engaging local populations in sustainable supply chain practices, businesses can create shared value and build long-term partnerships that benefit both the environment and society.

Recycling initiatives that involve communities are helping to address the growing waste crisis in African cities. Businesses are partnering with local organizations and residents to establish recycling programs that incentivize waste collection and segregation. For instance, a recycling company in Lagos could collaborate with schools and community groups to organize waste collection drives, providing participants with monetary rewards or educational materials in exchange for recyclables. These initiatives not only reduce waste but also raise awareness about sustainability at the grassroots level.

Indigenous communities often possess valuable knowledge and practices that contribute to environmental sustainability. Businesses can integrate this knowledge into their supply chain operations to promote sustainable practices while respecting local traditions. For example, a forestry company in Cameroon could work with indigenous communities to adopt sustainable logging methods that preserve biodiversity and protect cultural heritage. By recognizing and incorporating indigenous expertise, businesses can build trust and create inclusive supply chains that align with local values.

Regional cooperation is essential for scaling sustainability in African supply chains, as many challenges such as cross-border trade inefficiencies and resource management—require coordinated efforts across countries. Organizations such as the African Union and the African Continental Free Trade Area (AfCFTA) are providing platforms for collaboration and policy alignment.

One of the key areas for regional cooperation is the harmonization of sustainability standards and certifications. By aligning environmental and social standards across countries, regional bodies can simplify trade processes and encourage businesses to adopt sustainable practices. For instance, a regional certification program for sustainable agriculture could allow farmers in East Africa to access international markets more easily, boosting exports while promoting environmentally friendly practices.

Regional cooperation also facilitates the sharing of best practices, technologies, and resources among countries. For example, a knowledge-sharing initiative in Southern Africa could bring together businesses, governments, and non-governmental organizations to exchange insights on renewable energy adoption, circular supply chains, and community engagement. These exchanges enable stakeholders to learn from each other's experiences and accelerate the implementation of successful sustainability models.

Reviews

"A Transformative Blueprint for Africa's Supply Chains"
"The Role of Technology in Enhancing Supply Chain Visibility in Africa" is an exceptional piece of work that addresses one of the continent's most pressing economic challenges. Olajumoke Aroyewun combines in-depth research with practical insights, offering readers a clear roadmap for leveraging technology to revolutionize supply chains. This book is a must-read for policymakers, business leaders, and academics alike. It is both timely and visionary, providing solutions that are as practical as they are inspiring."
— Dr. Chinedu Obiora, Professor of Supply Chain Management, University of Lagos

"A Game-Changer for Business Innovation"
"This book is a game-changer for businesses operating in Africa. Aroyewun masterfully illustrates how emerging technologies such as AI, blockchain, and IoT are redefining supply chains, making them more efficient, transparent, and inclusive. The emphasis on sustainability and inclusivity makes this work even more impactful. It's a compelling read for anyone looking to navigate or invest in Africa's rapidly evolving business environment."
— Adaora Okonkwo, CEO, Global Logistics Solutions

"Practical, Insightful, and Inspirational"

"As someone actively involved in African trade, I found this book to be incredibly insightful and practical. The examples are relatable, and the strategies are actionable. Aroyewun's ability to combine technical expertise with a clear narrative is commendable. It's rare to find a book that is as accessible to professionals as it is to students and policymakers. This is a valuable resource for anyone interested in driving meaningful change in African supply chains."

— Musa Idris, Founder, Idris Agro-Logistics

"A Call to Action for a Sustainable Future"

"Olajumoke Aroyewun's book is not just an exploration of technology; it's a call to action for building sustainable and inclusive supply chains in Africa. The integration of real-world examples with forward-looking strategies makes it an essential guide for addressing the continent's unique challenges. This book is a reminder that Africa's economic transformation depends on embracing innovation, collaboration, and sustainability."

— Ngozi Adeyemi, Sustainability Advocate and Consultant

"A Must-Read for Africa's Future Leaders"

"This book stands out as an essential guide for the next generation of African leaders and innovators. Aroyewun provides a detailed yet engaging narrative on how technology can address systemic inefficiencies and foster economic growth. The focus on empowering communities and driving sustainability is particularly inspiring. It's a brilliant resource for anyone who believes in Africa's potential to lead on the global stage."

— Samuel Mensah, Policy Analyst, African Development Institute

Olajumoke Aroyewun